MW01680346

Mark-

I hope that you enjoy reading this book and that it might be helpful to you in putting together your story about South Pittsburg.

There's a rich history to our hometown.

I hope that you enjoy your stay here at the Hooch tonight!

You are welcome here now and in the future.

All the best to you!

Cheers!

Richard Rogers
12/2/2025

# Resilience, Tragedy, & Tenacity

# *Resilience, Tragedy, & Tenacity*

150 YEARS OF THE U.S. STOVE STORY
& THE FAMILY OF S.L. ROGERS, SR.

RICHARD ROGERS, FAMILY, FRIENDS,
AND EMPLOYEES OF U.S. STOVE

StoryTerrace

**Text** Daryn Kagan, on behalf of StoryTerrace

**Design** StoryTerrace

**Copyright** © The Rogers Family and StoryTerrace

**Text is private and confidential**

First print February 2022

StoryTerrace

www.StoryTerrace.com

# CONTENTS

*This is a story of success, tragedy, and adversity. Success that was mishandled leading to tragedy, tragedy overcome in the process of creating success.*

—Richard Rogers,
Chairman of the Board,
U.S. Stove

# INTRODUCTION: WHY TELL THIS STORY?

It was time.

It's as simple as that.

There sits in the southeastern corner of Tennessee a company and a family that has achieved success beyond most people's wildest dreams. They have also faced unbelievable challenges and tragedy. In the course of 150 years, this company has evolved, supporting families and a town.

On the occasion of the 150th anniversary of the U.S. Stove Company, the Rogers family decided it was time to share this story.

*The descendants of Stephen Leonard Rogers, Sr. & Ruth Parham Rogers gather for a family reunion. Summer 2021.*

During the summer of 2020, with the coronavirus pandemic holding the country captive, the family, friends, and employees got together through various ways to share what they know about how U.S. Stove came to be, weathered incredible challenges, and plans to grow into the future.

This book is for the family of U.S. Stove Co., the descendants of founder S.L. Rogers, Sr., the employees and multi-generational families who have worked for the company over the last 150 years. It's a mixture of interviews, research, Zoom calls, written recollections, and genealogy.

This is U.S. Stove, as seen by those who have known it, lived it, and loved it best.

# 1

# THE PLACE

To understand and appreciate the U.S. Stove story, you need to understand the geography and people of South Pittsburg, Tennessee. It's not the easiest place to live. The people who come from these jagged hills and steep terrain are tough. They are survivors, because they have had to be.

The Sequatchie Mountains frame South Pittsburg—tucking it between the Cumberland Plateau to the west and the Tennessee River to the east. Two steep ridges, Whitacre Point on the north and Lodge Point on the south, extend outwards from the Plateau to "wall in" the main portion of the city on the north, west, and south.

It sits 25 miles due west of Chattanooga, just where the Tennessee River decides to head south, right above the Alabama state line.

It is hard, jagged rock.

The river is wide, and the flow is strong.

The South Pittsburg Historic Preservation Society writes

that the Cherokee tribe were the first people to inhabit the area.

They lived there for thousands of years. By 1818, they had ceded their land to the state of Tennessee, and, along with hundreds of thousands of other Native Americans, were forced off the land and made to move to Oklahoma. This forced migration in the 1830s is known as "The Trail of Tears."

This is about the time that white settlers started moving into the area. They were mainly farmers who planted apple and peach orchards along the banks of the Tennessee River and up onto the slopes of the steep surrounding hills.

Both the Union and Confederate Armies used the area for camps during the Civil War. There were no major battles in the region, but it would be wrong to suggest that the land and the people didn't suffer as a result of the war. Soldiers from both sides trampled the area. They took advantage of local farmers helping themselves to food, crops, and livestock.

Rodger Castleberry was for many years the vice president of sales and marketing for U.S. Stove Company. He also became the unofficial company historian doing extensive research on the organization, the people, the family, and the area. Castleberry says you can't discount how tough these people were.

"This valley had been torn apart first by the Federal troops who invaded. Then, it was torn apart by the Confederate troops who pressed men into service and availed themselves of livestock, particularly horses and cattle. Once the war was over the place was devastated again by gangs. They raped, plundered, and pillaged the inhabitants. By the late 1800's, these are people who survived that. They did it with pioneer spirit and their basic strengths of spirit."

Except for outsiders who came to overrun the area, these were people basically cut off from the rest of the country. You might see some common last names running through this book. Castleberry explains the phenomenon.

"There were no roads through this area. Highway 41 did not exist. No one had ever heard of an interstate highway. There was so much inter-marriage, if not for the building of Hwy 41, the entire population would've died of hemophilia."

These were the people who, at the end of the Civil War, were once again facing the challenge of rebuilding their lives. The people of the region would have to fall back on their hardiness again to survive and rebuild their lives and area. To many, that meant heading into the coal mines that were starting to open in the area.

Soon after the war, investors saw a chance at prosperity with the building of the Jasper Branch Railroad. *The Tennessean* newspaper wrote on May 24, 1868, "The people of Sequatchie Valley are making vigorous efforts to extend the Jasper Branch Railroad to Pikeville."

The new railroad extension was everything to the growing coal industry. It meant new companies could get the coal out to bigger markets once miners had dug it out of the hills.

The area's first official post office, Battle Creek Mines, reflected the area's main industry at the time.

The growing industry put big ideas into some of the local leaders. They wouldn't have called it "marketing" then, but it surely falls under the idea of, *What's in a name?*

The idea was floated to rename the town, "South Pittsburg."

*A map of South Pittsburg, Tennessee*

They were dropping the "h" at the end, but the association would be immediate. This part of Tennessee, with its mineral deposits and growing industry and flowing river, would be seen as the "Pittsburgh of the South."

About this time, the seed for what would become U.S. Stove Company was being planted about a thousand miles away in Albany, New York. Perry Stove Works opened for business manufacturing and selling cast iron ranges and heaters.

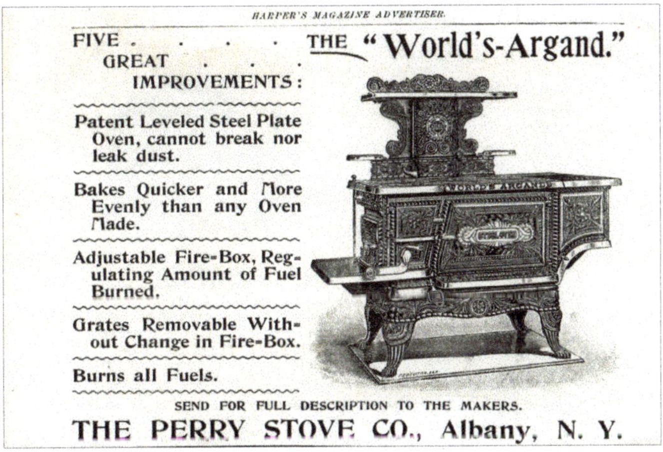


*An ad for the Perry Stove Company, the predecessor of the U.S. Stove Company.*

In 1886, the Perry Stove Works merged with Wetter Manufacturing and moved to Tennessee as the company looked to take advantage of the rich minerals and accessible transportation possibilities of the Tennessee River and the new railroad.

# 2

# THE HISTORY

In 2020, South Pittsburg's website celebrated its claim as, "The tidiest town in Tennessee." To be sure, the small city has long had much to offer, but this is a town with a challenging, sometimes bloody, past. Nothing tells this aspect of the story like the Christmas Day Massacre of 1927. The story sounds like something out of a Wild West movie, only this was a real-life bloody battle taking place.

The gun battle was the culmination of years of labor unrest. Henry Wetter wanted to run one of the biggest stove companies in the country as a non-union shop. The majority of the 400 workers wanted their union.

*Molders and foundry workers, South Pittsburg. 1925.*

On December 31, 1926 Wetter management shut out all the union workers. What followed was a year of court battles, picket lines, simmering disputes, and town power plays. By the end of 1927, South Pittsburg split in two; folks were either pro- or anti-union.

Middle Tennessee State University Professor Barbara Haskew's research showed that there were even two Christmas trees in town. The city put one up. The union put up the other.

By Christmas afternoon, 1927, things couldn't have been more tense. What started as a conversation to ease tensions ended in a bloody gun battle. By the time it was over, six men were dead, including the sheriff and police chief. Even after the shooting, things were so tense that Tennessee state troops had to be called in to restore order.

NASHVILLE TENNESSEAN

FIVE OFFICERS DIE IN MARION COUNTY BATTLE

Hickman Makes Two Attempts to End His Life

BEGINS JOURNEY TO LOS ANGELES TO FACE CHARGES

Accused Child Slayer Tries to Strangle Himself, Then Dives On His Head

YOUTH BROKEN

5 Believed Dead; Several Hurt As Fire Sweeps Hotel

NASHVILLE HOST TO SCIENTISTS; MEET TONIGHT

General Meeting to Be Held at War Memorial Building

ARRIVE TODAY

Foremost Authorities To Attend Sessions This Week

KIDNAPPING SCARE ENDS WHEN BOY IS FOUND NEAR JAIL

Christmas Wrecked for Glenn Nichols' Home; Spent Most of Day Downtown

CHRISTMAS BLAST KILLS 2 CHILDREN; THREE IN HOSPITAL

Clarence and Thaxton Swafford Victims

USES DYNAMITE

Father Tried to Find Firecracker Substitute

TROOPS SENT TO SOUTH PITTSBURG AFTER APPEAL

Chevrolet Plans To Announce New Line in January

Strike Feud Causes Night Gun Fight Between City And County Officers

LASTS MINUTE

Sheriff Killed During Clash; Chief of Police Is Believed Dying

*The headline of "The Nashville Tennessean" screams the news of the bloody battle on the streets of South Pittsburg.*

Today, you can still find exactly where the shootout took place. You'll find a historical marker at the corner of Cedar and Third Street in South Pittsburg. The mark it left on the town and hundreds of families and the region was so much bigger than a single metal plaque can convey.

*Historical marker in downtown South Pittsburg, TN, placed by South PIttsburg Historical Society.*

The shootout and labor strife left Wetter Stove Company in shambles. By 1931, Henry Wetter filed for bankruptcy, declaring, "I've had enough."

Over the next four years, a number of companies tried to come in and put the company back together again. None could get the stove company properly back on its feet.

In 1937, a man who some would say was the unlikeliest of success stories stepped in and reinvented the company as the U.S. Stove Company.

# 3

## S.L. ROGERS, SR.

Stephen Leonard Rogers was born in 1882 in Marion County, Tennessee, to Mary Francis Raulston and David Dame Rogers. Roger Castleberry points out that this was only seventeen years after the end of the Civil War. His childhood was anything but easy. David Rogers was the county sheriff, and, by many accounts, a violent alcoholic.

One-hundred and thirty-eight years later, Stephen's youngest daughter, Ruth, shares a story her father would sometimes tell her. "His father was what we would call today a binge drinker. He would get drunk, come home, and beat up on him."

*David Dame, Mary Prassie, Mary Francis, Stephen Leonard & Riley Clarence Rogers*

As her son grew, Stephen's mother, Francis, knew this would lead to a violent end if she didn't take drastic measures. She told young Stephen that he was going to have to leave home. "His mother made him leave home, because she was afraid that he'd kill his father if he came home again and started that. And she made him promise to never drink alcohol."

That's how sixteen-year-old Stephen Rogers headed out on his own. He stayed with relatives who owned a store in nearby Sweetens Cove. Rodger Castleberry shares some great stories about young Stephen:

"While staying with his relatives, Stephen heard there was hiring underway in Bridgeport, Alabama, at a factory that made handles. He walked the eight miles to the job site just to inquire about the opening and offer to do whatever needed to be done. The foreman in charge was impressed with the brash teenager, who showed grit. He hired Stephen right there on the spot, handing him a broom and shovel. His first job was sweeping up any dirt and dumping it in a large bin.

He lasted there a couple of years, long enough to become disillusioned with working in a factory. He found his second job a little closer to where he was staying at the Link Handle Factory in Sequatchie. He still had to figure out how to get to and from work 7 miles away, six days a week.

Teenager Stephen found his first mode of transportation riding an old mule. When that mule died, a coworker sold him a much younger mule for $7. That turned out to be quite the bargain, serving Stephen until he had saved enough money to buy his first automobile, a used Model T Ford."

*Stephen Leonard Rogers, Sr.*

Castleberry also points out that Stephen became a local hero in Sequatchie on April 5, 1911. He arrived early for work, despite a torrential downpour. Stephen noticed that the nearby Sequatchie River was rising very quickly, threatening to completely flood the Handle Works factory. Stephen was first to ring the alarm, then he started saving whatever he could. He sloshed through the deepening water, including the finished goods already packaged and ready for rail shipment to waiting customers. He used his Model T and some logging chains to drag, skid, and slip-slide those valuable handles—moving them to higher ground and under the roof of a vacant shed.

Stephen clearly had grit and ambition. He also had an ongoing challenge that threatened to stunt his ability to achieve great success. Leaving home at sixteen had also meant leaving school by the eighth grade, if not even sooner. If Stephen Rogers knew how to read or do simple math, he certainly didn't know how to do it well, a characteristic that hardly sounded like the making of a mogul. His fortunes changed for the better when he met Miss Amanda Raulston.

## Amanda Raulston Changes His Life

Amanda was seven years older than S.L. She was a school teacher when they met. *The Sequachee Valley News* announced her arrival at the local school February 6, 1902. "Miss Amanda Raulston of South Pittsburg, arrived Saturday night to take charge of the school and teach the secondary grade. She comes highly recommended having taught successfully at Whiteside, So. Pittsburg, and Tracy."

Did S.L. have an inkling that this young woman would be his wife? He certainly received a prediction early in 1902. *The Sequachee Valley News* carried an item describing a party in March of that year. "A surprise and tacky party held sway at the home of William Houts Saturday night for a few merry hours. Miss Malthide Gustafson told fortunes and all of the boys will get married within six months."

Stephen is listed as one of the guests attending the party at the Houts family home. That was March. He and Amanda Raulston were married in July, five months after her arrival in town.

In that short amount of time, Amanda appears to have secured a promotion.

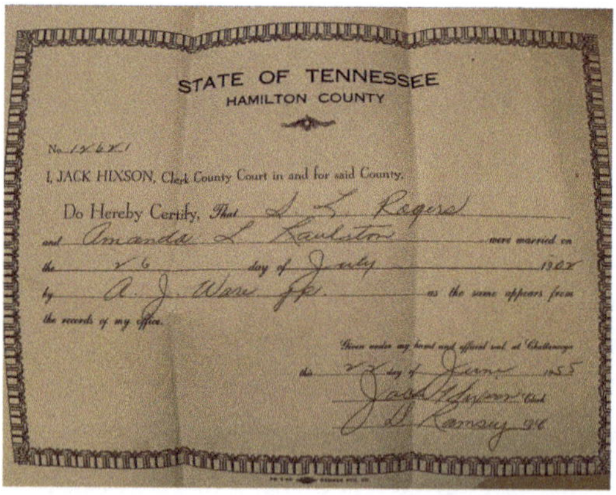
STATE OF TENNESSEE
HAMILTON COUNTY

No. [illegible]

I, JACK HIXSON, Clerk County Court in and for said County,

Do Hereby Certify, That S. L. Rogers and Amanda L. Raulston were married on the 26 day of July 1902 by A. J. Ware J.P. as the same appears from the records of my office.

Given under my hand and official seal at Chattanooga this [illegible] day of June 1955

Jack Hixson Clerk
J. D. Ramsey D.C.

*Stephen Leonard Rogers, Sr. & Amanda L. Raulston's Marriage Certificate*

"Mr. Leonard Rogers of this city and Miss Amanda Raulston of Anderson, Tenn., were married at the Read House in Chattanooga, Sunday, July 26. They will make their home at this place where the groom has an important position with the Sequachee Handle Works. The bride is the principal of the Sequachee Public School and had a very successful term this spring." Stephen was nineteen years old. Amanda was 26.

The newspaper announcement uses Stephen's middle name, "Leonard." Through much of his life, he did use his middle name of Leonard, a name his future son would also go by. For purposes of this book, we will refer to him as Stephen or S.L., Sr.

What can you make out of the fact that Stephen married a woman with the same maiden name as his mother? Did he marry his cousin? Did he know of her before she started teaching school in South Pittsburg? We don't know the exact answer. Great granddaughter, Stephanie Rogers Esper, did some research to find that Amanda and S.L. were indeed related. S.L.'s maternal grandfather, John Simmons Raulston (1824–1906) was the brother of Amanda's paternal grandfather, Samuel Raulston (1810–1866.)

Most importantly, Amanda taught her young husband the reading and math skills he needed to back up the big dreams burning inside him. He was born to be an entrepreneur long before such a word was in fashion. S.L. Rogers knew one thing for sure: He was destined to be more than labor and toil for someone else's company and profits.

His daughter, Ruth, points out that Amanda taught him even more than letters and numbers. "She taught him manners, basically, everything he needed to know in life. His mother and father were pretty backwoods and not terribly educated people. He was a country boy from the backwoods, who had a brilliant mind. Amanda brought that out a lot."

Within the first year of their marriage, Stephen and Amanda moved to South Pittsburg, where he began work at the H. Wetter Manufacturing, the company that would one day become the U.S. Stove Company.

By 1903, he was working as a molder. This would have entailed long hours doing a dirty and dangerous job. Grandson Richard Rogers knows it well. He did the same job 70 years later; even then, it had not yet changed very much.

To be a molder involved working from early in the morning until mid-afternoon shoveling sand into a flask containing a pattern made of aluminum. The sand was then packed manually using an assortment of tools. The completed molds were then set into place to be poured full of molten iron in the afternoon. It was back-breaking and hot, dirty work.

Grandson Richard will always remember wearing special boots that had a leather loop above the heel. "It was there in case you poured hot metal down your boot. Using that loop to get your boot off in an instant would be the only hope you had of saving your foot." That's something Richard learned firsthand when he survived a frightening incident as a young man. The molten iron pouring into his boot about cost him his foot. The loop on the heel of his boot and some quick thinking saved the day and Richard's foot.

Richard points out that his grandfather would have been working under piecework conditions. He would have toiled all those long, hard, dangerous hours only getting paid for the pieces that later passed inspection.

## Setting Out, Natural Entrepreneur

Stephen Leonard Rogers worked seven long years saving up enough money and putting himself in position to start his first company. By 1910, S.L. Rogers was running an undertaking and livery business 20 miles north of South Pittsburg in Whitwell.

Undertaking speaks for itself. What is "livery?" Think of it as the precursor of a rental car business like Avis or Hertz: carriages or vehicles for hire. By 1918, S.L. was showing that his business was one to watch. He bought the first motor-powered hearse to be put into service in Marion County. The local funeral trade was never the same again.

This is also about the time that Stephen Rogers got his first taste of local politics—serving as Trustee of Marion County and as the Marion County Road Commissioner. During his last and third term as road commissioner, he took over the Whitwell Coal Company.

Daughter Ruth remembers, "He referred to running for office as 'electioneering.' He told stories of his travels around the county and of spending nights with folks along the way. He loved to tell stories, such as a night he spent when he had to sleep in bed with two other men, one of whom chewed tobacco and spit straight up. He was always telling me stories—some true and some fanciful."

S.L.'s stepping into public office was not without controversy. A letter he wrote to be published in the local newspaper in 1916 indicates that he believed there were voting irregularities.

"To the Republicans of Marion Co.," he opened. "When I entered the contest in the recent Republican primary election for the nomination of the Trustee of Marion County, I did so with the knowledge that all the candidates except one would be defeated and I might be among the defeated ones. Had I been defeated my full intention was to give my hearty support to the candidate who defeated me.

For some reason or cause the returns from Mt. Olivet on the mountain above Whitwell was not forwarded to the county chairman, but with this box out of the count, the return showed that I received a plurality of eighty-three votes over my leading competitor, and it seems to me that I should have been declared the Republican nominee for Trustee."

S.L. goes on to cast disapproval of how the situation

was handled and investigated and seems to say he has no choice but to declare himself the official nominee. "After considering the matter carefully, I feel I am the nominee of the republican party as fully as if I had been declared so by the Chairman and Secretary, and as such, have the right to make the race before the people of Marion County.

In announcing myself to be a candidate to be voted for in the August election, I appeal to the loyal republicans throughout the county and also to my democratic friends for their hearty support."

S.L. 's daring gamble to self-declare himself his party's nominee paid off, as he pulled off an upset in that August election.

"The results of the election last Thursday were peculiar. John A. Hoge, a Democrat, who was believed to be the favorite for trustee, lost the race by 47 votes to S.L. Rogers, a Republican."

S. L. Rogers' life in public service was launched. He served as trustee for Marion County for three terms and another three terms as the Marion County Road Commissioner.

During his last term as Road Commissioner, he had the chance to take over the Whitwell Coal Company. The company was $44,000 in debt. Where others might have seen a mess, S.L. saw an opportunity. He also saw that no one builds a successful business by himself. He gave huge praise for the people who helped him turn the business around. He especially gave credit to his best salesman, Wilkes Thrasher, who developed huge connections and accounts for the Whitwell coal in Chattanooga.

These early forays into the coal business were a chance for S.L. to use his natural management skills. Rodger Castleberry says S.L. was a natural leader, and, in more modern terms, a people person. "In the 1920s, the union movement was moving through the South.

In two different heated situations, S.L. was able to mollify the men, the companies, and union, hence his coal operations were successful. From management he was able to advance to ownership of at least two of these coal mines."

## Tragedy Strikes

While Stephen was clearly his own man in the business world, tragedy struck. In 1922, his wife, Amanda, died after a brief illness. Her death certificate indicates she died of an abdominal infection following a ruptured ovarian cyst. Stephen Rogers was almost 40 years old, a widower with no children.

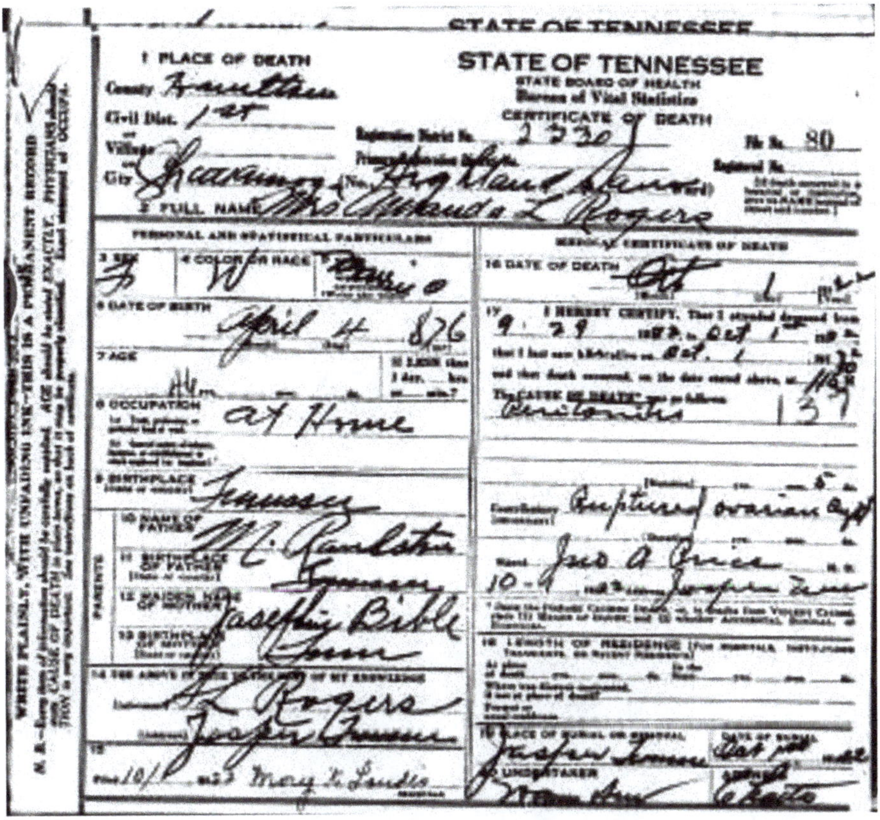
STATE OF TENNESSEE

1 PLACE OF DEATH

STATE OF TENNESSEE
STATE BOARD OF HEALTH
Bureau of Vital Statistics
CERTIFICATE OF DEATH

File No. 80

2 FULL NAME Mrs Amanda L Rogers

PERSONAL AND STATISTICAL PARTICULARS

MEDICAL CERTIFICATE OF DEATH

16 DATE OF DEATH

6 DATE OF BIRTH April 4 1876

7 AGE

8 OCCUPATION at Home

9 BIRTHPLACE

10 NAME OF FATHER

12 MAIDEN NAME OF MOTHER Josephine Bible

14 THE ABOVE IS TRUE TO THE BEST OF MY KNOWLEDGE

A L Rogers

18 LENGTH OF RESIDENCE

19 PLACE OF BURIAL OR REMOVAL

DATE OF BURIAL

UNDERTAKER

*Amanda Raulston Rogers' death certificate lists her cause of death as "peritonitis," inflammation of the abdomen lining.*

# A New Family

His chance to find love again happened at a party in Chattanooga. Daughter Ruth believes her uncle gets some credit for her parents' match. Grady Parham was a successful businessman in Chattanooga, having started the Red Food Store grocery store chain. He threw the party where Stephen Rogers met Grady's sister, Ruth, who was 25 years old at the time.

*Ruth Parham Rogers, 1923.*

Their wedding announcement, which ran June 14, 1924 in the *Nashville Banner*, gives details that can make you feel like you were there.

"The wedding of Miss Ruth Parham and Stephen Leonard Rogers of Chattanooga was beautifully solemnized Monday afternoon at 4 o'clock at the home of the bride in the presence of a company of 60 relatives and friends.

The house was decorated with a number of rambler roses, ferns and palms. The ceremony was performed before an improvised altar of ferns and palms banked before the fireplace in the living room."

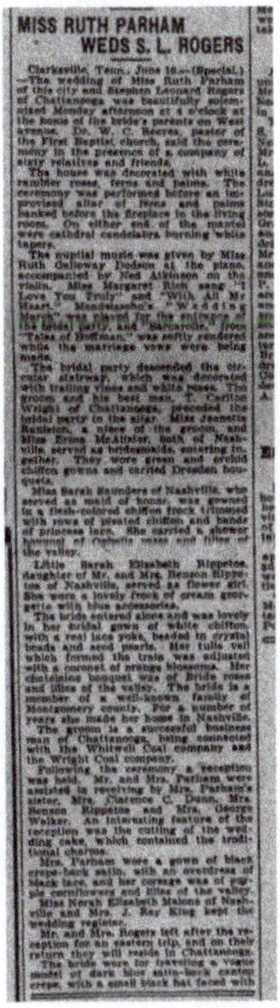

**MISS RUTH PARHAM WEDS S. L. ROGERS**

Clarksville, Tenn., June 16.—(Special.)—The wedding of Miss Ruth Parham of this city and Stephen Leonard Rogers of Chattanooga was beautifully solemnized Monday afternoon at 4 o'clock at the home of the bride's parents on West avenue. Dr. W. C. Reeves, pastor of the First Baptist church, said the ceremony in the presence of a company of sixty relatives and friends.

The house was decorated with white rambler roses, ferns and palms. The ceremony was performed before an improvised altar of ferns and palms banked before the fireplace in the living room. On either end of the mantel were cathedral candelabra burning white tapers.

The nuptial music was given by Miss Ruth Galloway Dodson at the piano, accompanied by Ned Atkinson on the violin. Miss Margaret Rich sang "I Love You Truly" and "With All My Heart." Mendelssohn's "Wedding March" was played for the entrance of the bridal party, and "Barcarole," from "Tales of Hoffman," was softly rendered while the marriage vows were being made.

The bridal party descended the circular stairway, which was decorated with trailing vines and white roses. The groom and his best man, T. Carlton Wright of Chattanooga, preceded the bridal party to the altar. Miss Jeanette Hamleton, a niece of the groom, and Miss Erma McAlister, both of Nashville, served as bridesmaids, entering together. They wore green and orchid chiffon gowns and carried Dresden bouquets.

Miss Sarah Saunders of Nashville, who served as maid of honor, was gowned in a flesh-colored chiffon frock trimmed with rows of pleated chiffon and bands of princess lace. She carried a shower bouquet of Ophelia roses and lilies of the valley.

Little Sarah Elizabeth Rippetoe, daughter of Mr. and Mrs. Benson Rippetoe of Nashville, served as flower girl. She wore a lovely frock of cream georgette with blue accessories.

The bride entered alone and was lovely in her bridal gown of white chiffon, with a real lace yoke, beaded in crystal beads and seed pearls. Her tulle veil which formed the train was adjusted with a coronet of orange blossoms. Her chatelaine bouquet was of Bride roses and lilies of the valley. The bride is a member of a well-known family of Montgomery county. For a number of years she made her home in Nashville.

The groom is a successful business man of Chattanooga, being connected with the Whitwell Coal company and the Wright Coal company.

Following the ceremony a reception was held. Mr. and Mrs. Parham were assisted in receiving by Mrs. Parham's sister, Mrs. Clarence C. Dunn, Mrs. Benson Rippetoe and Mrs. George Walker. An interesting feature of the reception was the cutting of the wedding cake, which contained the traditional charms.

Mrs. Parham wore a gown of black crepe-back satin, with an overdress of black lace, and her corsage was of purple cornflowers and lilies of the valley.

Miss Norah Elizabeth Malone of Nashville and Mrs. J. Ray King kept the wedding register.

Mr. and Mrs. Rogers left after the reception for an eastern trip, and on their return they will reside in Chattanooga.

The bride wore for traveling a vogue model of dark blue satin-back canton crepe, with a small black hat faced with

*The Chattanooga News reports the 1924 wedding of Ruth Parham and S.L.R., Sr.*

Tucked into this wedding announcement was the smallest clue that though S.L. was starting a new life with Ruth, he still had close ties to Amanda's family. "Miss Jeanette Raulston, a niece of the groom served as a bridesmaid." Great-granddaughter Stephanie Esper is the Rogers family genealogist. She discovered that Jeanette Raulston was the daughter of Amanda's brother.

Daughter Ruth believes including this connection to his first wife would be something her mother would have wanted, even pushed for. She says, "It would have been just like my mother to want to show respect for Amanda."

It's clear that S.L. wanted everything to be perfect for his wedding to Ruth. Here is a glimpse from his personal diary showing his precise checklist to make sure the day went off without a hitch.

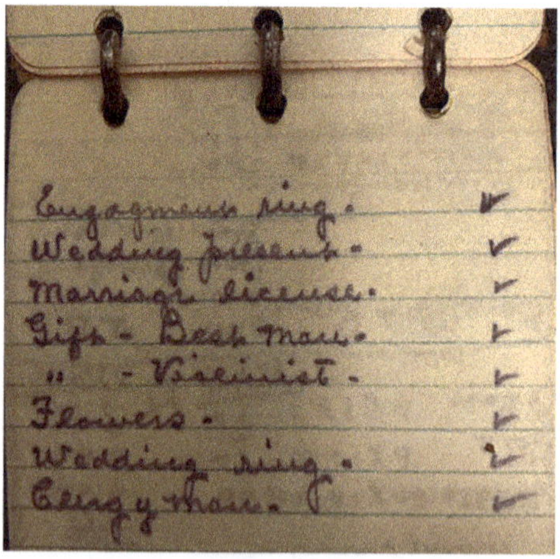

Engagement ring.
Wedding present.
Marriage license.
Gift - Best man.
" - Violinist.
Flowers.
Wedding ring.
Clergyman.

*S.L.R., Sr.'s handwritten "To Do" checklist for his 1924 wedding to Ruth Parham.*

The announcement wrapped up with a few more tidbits on what life was going to look like for the new couple. "Mr. and Mrs. Rogers left after the reception for an eastern tour and on their return will be located in Chattanooga.

The bride is a member of a well-known Montgomery County family.

The groom is a successful businessman being connected with the Whitwell Coal Company and Wright Coal Company."

Another announcement in the "Chattanooga News" provided even more details that make the wedding come to life.

There was live music featuring a pianist and a violinist. "Miss Margaret Rich sang 'I Love You Truly' and 'With All My Heart.' Mendelssohn's 'Wedding March' was played for the entrance of the wedding party and 'Barcarolle' from 'Tales of Hoffman' was softly rendered while the marriage vows were being made."

There are a few clues that 25-year-old Ruth had an independent streak as she entered into marriage. "The bride entered alone and was lovely in a bridal gown of white chiffon with a real lace yoke beaded in crystal beads and seed pearls. Her tulle veil, which formed the train, was adjusted with a coronet of orange blossoms. Her chatelaine bouquet was of Bride roses and lily of the valley. For a number of years, the bride made her home in Nashville."

One more interesting tidbit from the *Chattanooga News*

item shares that the mother of the bride actually wore black to her daughter's wedding. "Mrs. Parham wore a gown of black crepe-back satin with an overdress of black lace and her corsage was of purple cornflowers and lilies of the valley."

*The Chattanooga News* piece makes note of the wedding cake.

"An interesting feature of the reception was the cutting of the wedding cake which contained the traditional charms."

Placing charms on ribbons inside a wedding cake is a Southern tradition that works much like throwing the bouquet. Gambinos.com explains that the bride has her wedding party gather around the cake. Each young woman picks a ribbon. On cue, they each pull their ribbon at the same time, exposing a charm that is meant to predict the puller's future.

There are eight classic charms historically used for ribbon pulls, each with its own meaning. The ring indicates who will be next to get married. The horseshoe or the four-leaf clover signifies good luck. The telephone predicts good news is on the way. The anchor offers encouraging hope. The heart indicates love is on the way. The thimble or button sadly predicts the woman will be an old maid, and a penny indicates poverty.

# A Family Is Born: The Four Rogers Children

*Stephen Leonard Rogers, Jr., Emma Lockert Rogers, Nancy Jane Rogers & Ruth Parham Rogers.*

The new couple started their life together in Whitwell, Tennessee. They would eventually move to Chattanooga, then to a farm in South Pittsburg, and eventually to what was affectionately known as "The Big House."

By 1924, Stephen and Ruth had started building their family. Their first child, Stephen Leonard Rogers, Jr., was born the next year. With that, Stephen became S.L. Rogers, Sr. Even more importantly, he took on a job he'd long wanted. He became a father.

Ruth shares, "My mother said that when my brother was

born, my father went around in a daze for at least a week. He just could not believe he had a son. He had gotten to the promised land."

Three daughters made life even better. Emma arrived in 1927. Nancy Jane was born in 1930. Their third daughter was born nine years later in 1939, becoming the third generation to be given the name of Ruth.

As for the nine-year gap between babies, it did not go unnoticed. Ruth remembered, "I got a confession out of my mother that I was an accident. An anniversary celebration, I think. Yeah. June to March, it figures you know? Though they never made me feel that way."

The nine-year gap meant a new era for this family. Ruth was the first and only of the Rogers children to be born in a hospital, rather than at home.

Even with all the children, it appears there was room for more. Ruth Parham's mother came to live with her daughter's family. This tidbit reveals itself in Emma Lockert Parham's obituary, which appeared in the *Leaf-Chronicle* newspaper September 7, 1942. "Mrs. Parham had made her home with her daughter, Mrs. S.L. Rogers of South Pittsburg, Tenn. since the death of her husband 10 years ago."

## U.S. Stove Is Born

While S.L. and Ruth were busy building their family, he was also busy expanding his business interests. In addition to the coal mines in Whitwell, Victoria, and Daus, he had farming and livestock interests throughout the area. In 1936, some community leaders approached him about taking on what appeared to be another business disaster.

Over the previous ten years, three teams had tried to raise the old Wetter Stove company from the ashes of the years of labor disputes and lawsuits. Even to a turnaround specialist like S.L., this didn't sound like a fabulous idea. On one hand, he knew only too well the years of squabbling and bickering, not to mention the tragedy of the Christmas Day Massacre.

On the other hand, he had personal ties to the company, having once worked as a molder's assistant in one of his early jobs. Here were a number of community leaders imploring him to take this on, not just as a business opportunity, but rather, as a business leader. His turning around this decade-long mess could have incredible economic benefits for South Pittsburg, not to mention the healing it could bring to the community.

S.L. finally agreed. He came up with a plan to revive the business under the new banner, "The United States Stove Company."

S.L.'s future son-in-law, Bob Thomas, would later write

that it was T.R. Preston, the president of Hamilton National Bank, who called S.L. asking him to buy the about-to-be-bankrupt business. "S.L. sold his house and all his assets except a thousand acres he had on the side of the mountain at Dunlap—most everything he had to buy the company."

Bob Thomas was clearly impressed by the risk and reward. "S.L. Rogers built U.S. Stove into a multi-million-dollar business."

*U.S. Stove foundry workers pour hot iron into molds to produce stove parts.*

That was clearly no easy task. David Head wrote in the *South Pittsburg Marion Hustler* newspaper, "Taking over the U.S. Stove Company proved to be a daunting task. Starting up a mothballed industry in the grips of The Great Depression would have been a challenge for any man but S.L. was no ordinary man! He took off the gloves and soon had the business on an even keel. Blood, sweat, and tears paid off and by the end of the Depression the United States Stove Company was turning a profit, albeit a small one. A 1937 contract with Sears would last 37 years and account for three-quarters of the company's volume. The United States Stove Company would also wholesale their stoves to Montgomery Ward, Spiegel, Aldens, and numerous furniture and hardware distributors.

*"The Big House" in South Pittsburg, TN, Ruth Rogers' dream house. The family moved here in the mid-1940's.*

The family moved to the Col. Downing home at the corner of Fourth Street and Magnolia Avenue once the children finished school at Chattanooga. The Rogers' family purchased the home and lived there for many years. When World War II came along the company's stoves were shipped to our armed forces all over the world. It was cold on the Eastern Front and the stoves were a godsend."

## Smart Moves

S.L. reorganized the company debt to be paid off over a fifteen-year period, from 1937–1952. Like many of his business goals, S.L. wound up blowing that target away. U.S. Stove Company paid off that debt four years early in 1948. The company proved to be a good bet for investors. Preferred stockholders who invested in the new corporation received $1.87 for every dollar invested.

Castleberry believes one of S.L.'s first moves with U.S. Stove was his most important and smartest. He hired his cousin, J. Leonard "Ram" Raulston, a man who had big plans that didn't include living in South Pittsburg, where he had grown up.

Raulston was a University of Tennessee law school graduate who dreamed of setting up a law practice in Chattanooga, but S.L. was able to persuade him to join him in this venture of trying to resurrect this dormant company.

"S.L. was the people person. He handled the inside,

rewarding people, patting them on the back. Raulston was more of an outside guy, brilliant at sales. Together they performed some miracles."

One of their first moves involved a unique approach to giving and selling stock in the new company. They reached out to vendors and merchants who had suffered financially when the old Harvest Company declared bankruptcy. These offers were quickly accepted.

Another lucky break occurred when Raulston remembered one of his buddies from law school was the son of an executive at Sears & Roebuck Company. He was able to get an introduction and, incredibly, sold U.S. Stove into the Sears & Roebuck Fall catalog for 1938.

The book featured a parlor stove, two sizes of a magazine coal heater, and the Model 26 Logwood Box Heater; each of those was made from patterns dating to Harvest Stove Company days.

Rodger Castleberry says Leonard Raulston had his own method of selling to the company's main customer, Sears Roebuck. "Once a year, Raulston would head to Chicago to meet with the Sears folks. On the way he'd stop by Louisville, Kentucky, and meet with men who owned and ran local hardware stores. He'd say, 'I'm fixing to go up here to Chicago and sell the inventory of the company out. If you need anything you need to tell me right now.'"

S.L. was a hard worker who demanded the same from everyone who worked for him.

Grandson Richard Rogers shares, "I've heard stories about him, walking through the plant; if somebody wasn't working hard enough, he just grabbed them by the shirt collar, threw them out the door, and would say, 'Hey you ain't working hard enough, get out of here.'

*A U.S. Stove employee operates a drill press on a cast iron door for a wood stove.*

He smoked these big cigars, and when the employees smelled cigar smoke, they would pick up the pace, because they knew that the old man—SL Sr., he's around the corner."

As the U.S. Stove Company grew, so did the other Rogers businesses. Marion Lumber provided the crates for all the stoves to be shipped in. It also inspired a housing boom around the Valley. An ad from the South Pittsburg Hustler newspaper in 1941 makes the case for owning and building your own home.

"Want a home like this one?" it reads. "You can have it for your very own! Yes, if you earn an average salary you can earn the home you've always wanted, at far less cost than you might imagine. You and your family will live far happier lives in a home of your own and as long as it is so easy to do, you owe it to yourself to investigate. We can furnish all materials from the foundation to the roof!"

## Fatherhood

While S.L. was surely busy building his business empire, he also invested in a job he adored, being a father. Ruth remembers a father who "was always interested in what I was interested in. He would keep me company when he returned home from work when I was sick and tell me stories and play with me. He seemed to know the best thing to say in a situation. I always loved to crawl up and sit in his lap.

He was a loving father, who provided well and thoughtfully for all of us."

He showed his love and interest by sparking fun. Ruth remembered that he taught her how to play poker, something a lot of girls in South Pittsburg, Tennessee, certainly were not learning in the 1940s.

Ruth sums up her father this way: "He has simply been the role model for my life. I think it has to do with being honest, with working hard for what you want in your life. It has to do with being compassionate. It has to do with 'I have always known that I was loved.' And he's the one who did it. I look back and think, *Wow what a gift that he gave.* All three of us sisters were talking once, when Emma said, 'I know I was the favorite child.' Then Nancy said, 'No, he told me I was the favorite child.' And I said, 'He didn't have to tell me, I know I'm his favorite.' So, he did that. He was just that kind of caring person; made each of us feel like we were his favorite."

So, there was a debate among the girls about who was the favorite daughter. There was no debate as to the favorite son. There was only one. S.L. Rogers, Jr., or Leonard, or Lenny, as he was known for most of his life. Ruth always understood that the relationship between father and son was different than the one Senior had with his daughters.

"He was very strict with Leonard. My mother said it was just different. She said that the one time he hit him, Leonard was just a little boy. He was just two or three years old. He'd spilled something or made some other mistake, and our dad spanked him on the legs. Mother said, 'I didn't like it, but I didn't say anything.' I think that's how he was treated by his own father."

The family moved around the area over the years, mainly to provide the best opportunity for the four children. They moved from Whitwell to Chattanooga in the 1930s, so the older three children could go to better schools. They moved to Kimball to a farm just off US 41 in the early 40s.

In the middle 40s, they bought one of the oldest houses in South Pittsburg, what came to be known as "The Big House," sitting on the corner of Magnolia and Fourth Street. The house became the center of Rogers Family life, serving as the backdrop for family events and memories that many generations remember.

*S.L.Rogers, Sr (sitting in middle) with "little" Ruth Rogers on his lap, Ruth Rogers (standing behind him on right.)*

# Becoming Mayor

# [...]tsburg Hustler

DEVOTED TO THE INTERESTS OF SOUTH PITTSBURG, MARION COUNTY, AND SEQUATCHIE VALLEY

[...], TENN., THURSDAY, DECEMBER 16, 1948 — NUMBER 51

## ALL SAVE ONE ROGERS-KELLERMANN TICKET SWEPT INTO OFFICE

### The Incoming and Outgoing

S. L. ROGERS

OUTGOING MAYOR R. A. Padgett, shown above, was first elected as the city's chief executive on Monday, December 12, 1932, defeating the incumbent, R. C. Aycock by 18 votes. Padgett received 493 votes to Aycock's 475. Padgett had served for a time as Commissioner of Finance and Health. Serving on the board at that time were R. C. Aycock, R. A. Padgett, August Patton, Ambrose Acklen, R. L. Lodge. This was the year when the latter dropped out and Ray S. Reiling was elected to take his post. Thus it will be seen that Mayor Padgett has served at the head of city government for 15 consecutive years, during which time there have come many achievements. Among these might be mentioned the city's refinancing plan whereby a tremendous

### BRIEF HISTORY OF OUR NEW MAYOR

STEPHEN LEONARD ROGERS is 66 years of age. He is a son of the late Sheriff David D. Rogers and Frances Raulston Rogers, was born one mile north of Pleasant Grove and has spent his entire life in Marion County. He received his early training in the elementary schools of his community, later attended Sam Houston Academy and also Pryor Institute, the latter place of learning now known as Marion County High School.

His first work was with the Sequatchie Handle Works under the late G. Sherman. This was in the year 1898. It was while engaged here that he was married to Miss Amanda Raulston and with his bride he came to South Pittsburg in 1902 where he began work under the late W. H. Gurney, veteran stove foundry superintendent. This was the beginning of a successful stove career.

More specifically was his stove career marked a year later when he began his molding trade in what was then called the "little shop" just south of the main plant of the H. Wetter Manufacturing Company when a number of young men joined him at their respective benches. The writer was among this group and as we recall it there were three and possibly others. One of these was A. R. (Daddy) Williamson and the others, Clark and Charles Huntington. The former returned to his trade in the printing office, Williamson entered the drug business and the Huntington boys went back to Memphis from whence they came.

Rogers, or Mayor-elect Rogers, if you please, stuck it out seven years, during which time he became chairman of the local AF of L price committee. And it was during this time that he came to know the real problems of the working man which has served him in many ways in recent years when his problems have been multiplied over and over again and his obligations to labor have mounted from a mole hill to a mountain.

Ambitious as most men of his type are at that age, he left the molding trade and went to Whitwell and bought the undertaking and livery business operated there at the time by the late J. J. Dykes and J. H. Northcut. He made a success of this venture and in 1916 made a successful race against the late J. A. Hoge for Trustee of Marion County which office he held for three terms of two years each. He was defeated by B. Holloway and this was in 1922. His term of office expired on September 1, 1922, and his wife died exactly one month later. To this union there was no issue.

Two years later and on June 9, 1924, Mr. Rogers was again married, this time to Miss Ruth Parham of Clarksville. This union has been blessed with four children and they are Stephen Leonard, Jr., Emma Lockert, Nancy Jane and Ruth Parham Rogers.

At the expiration of his three terms as trustee, he went to Morganville in the upper end of Marion County where he took over the Whitwell Coal Company which had gone into bankruptcy a short time before owing a heavy bond[e]d indebtedness. This he was successful in paying off, after wh[ic]h he bought the mines and put them back on a paying basis. In addition to his mine operations, he was also engaged in far[ming] and livestock raising which he later gave up to take over a second bankruptcy, [this] time the United States Stove Corporation.

The above corporation failed, owin[g] a very large bond[ed in]debtedness. Something in the neighborhood of $150,000.00 [...] physical properties had long been neglected until the task of b[ring]ing the plant back to its peak days seemed an impossible one, [but] with his outstanding ability and with the cooperation of his ex[cel]lent office group and an understanding force of men in every department who have learned to know and respect him, President Rogers has pulled the old ship of state safely to anchor and in addition to making this one of the largest and best stove manufacturing concerns to be found anywhere in the South, it is the un[der]standing of this newspaper that other additions and improv[e]ments are in the offing.

And may it be said of President Rogers, who is our M[ayor-]elect, that he has never been the man to appropriate unto [himself] credit for the successes made. He inevitably insists th[...] wear the laurels and that he will gladly share that [...]

### ROGERS WINS OVER ANDERSON WITH A SURPRISING MARGIN

KELLERMAN, FOR STREET JOB MAKES SPLENDID SHOWING

Gibson, Only Man On Rogers Ticket Nosed Out, Beaten By Roy Sanders, Jr., With a Vote of 475 to 469 — Beene, Honey Have Majorities.

The highly enthused city election passed into history as one of the smoothest, most orderly ever held in South Pittsburg and long before the final count was tabulated it became evident that the so-called Rogers ticket was in for a win. Even at that time the race between some of the candidates was nip and tuck and as many as three times some of the candidates were tied. But the final score was as follows:

For Mayor, Jasper (Jap) Anderson, 374; Leonard Rogers, 601, making the latter's majority 227.

For Finance Commissioner, Philip Beene, 470; George Wiesener, 446, a majority for Beene of 24 votes.

For Police Commissioner, Richard Gibson, 469; Roy Sanders, Jr., 475. This gave Sanders a lead of 6 votes and added up to the closest of the races.

For Street Commissioner, Leslie Kellermann, 560; Herschel Matthews, 374. Kellermann's majority 186.

For Health [redacted]
rence Honey, [redacted]
374 and this ga[redacted]
jority.

Readers of [redacted]
too well famil[redacted]
of Monday's [redacted]
comment. It [redacted]
state for the [redacted]
for some reas[redacted]
get these det[redacted]

*Stephen Leonard Rogers, Sr.; The Mayor of South Pittsburg, Tennessee. Taken from The SP Hustler.*

S.L. Rogers became mayor of South Pittsburg in January 1949. He addressed the new city commissioners—stating his intentions and expectations as he took over the helm of the city.

"First. I shall insist on placing men in key positions who are capable and efficient in the discharge of their duties, also willing to give the time and thought necessary for having a progressive program for the city, regardless of political affiliations."

"Second. I shall insist on the installation of a modern accounting system in order that the affairs of the city may run in a businesslike manner."

"Third. I shall invite criticism so long as it is constructive and will have no patience with any other kind."

"Fourth. I shall use the same procedure with reference to the individuals or delegations as I have used in dealing with the employees of the U.S. Stove Co. during the twelve years I have been in charge—any and all citizens of the city will be given a courteous hearing whether or not we will be able to agree. Our plant had been subjected to some unfavorable publicity in the past, and I have always insisted on keeping our differences housed within our walls."

"Fifth. I shall recommend to you that all employees be paid a reasonable salary for their services and demand of them efficient service and a full accounting to the board."

Niece Stephanie Rogers Esper sums up her great grandfather: "He wasn't just U.S. Stove. He was in the coal mining business, and he was the mayor of South Pittsburg. He obviously had amazing people skills. He knew how to treat people. And so, to me, that is very telling just how he was able to move people, to inspire people to do great things."

It's clear Mayor Rogers felt an obligation to the citizens of South Pittsburg. After his first year in office, he created a letter, a report of sorts, describing the progress he and his administration had made in running the city. "As mayor of your city, I feel it is my duty to give an account of what has been accomplished by my present commission during the first year of our administration."

Mayor Rogers started out by explaining that he believed in delegating leadership and responsibility to the young men running various departments. "This board is composed of young men with the exception of myself. They are men whose integrity is above criticism."

He went on to describe how the budget was based on previous tax collections, showing that he valued a balanced budget. When the city found an unexpected bounty of even more tax dollars collected, Mayor Rogers ordered that money distributed to various departments.

Some of that money went to the police department. Police Commissioner Roy Sanders, Jr. used the money to keep his officers well paid. Mayor Rogers also reported that the extra money allowed the commissioner to "purchase a modern fire engine and make substantial repairs to City Hall."

The Department of Streets was able to build "five new concrete bridges replacing wooden structures, a network of unobstructed alleys; installation of several hundred feet of drainage tile, including the line recently installed in our high school; a power mowing machine, which, when not used in approving appearance of our city streets, may be secured for private use at reasonable cost by any citizen of South Pittsburg."

The mayor also reported that Commissioner of Health, Lawrence Honey, was hoping to soon be able to improve sanitary conditions in the city.

Daughter Ruth remembers her father having a clear ethical sense as mayor. "There was this pompous and arrogant man who was one of the officials in the Mayor's office who got a parking ticket. My dad happened to pull up when he said, 'Can you see this?' suggesting he shouldn't have to deal with such punishments and inconveniences. I remember Papa stroking his chin and saying, 'You go pay that parking ticket. You don't get any special privileges just because you're on the board.'"

S.L. Rogers' mayoral career came to an end in a most unusual way. Integrity was at play, a word that often trips up many politicians. This story played out in a way you don't hear much about in modern times.

In 1955, there was great interest in bringing a large textile mill to South Pittsburg. Textiles had been part of the town's economy as early as the 1920s. R.P. Shapard, owner of the Spaulding Knitting Mill in Griffin, Georgia, suggested that if a big enough facility could be built, they would be interested in relocating to South Pittsburg. The facility would employ as many as 200 people with an annual payroll of $500,000.

Such an operation would be a huge boon to the local economy; even more so, the addition of this type of mill was seen as an opportunity for the city to finally live up to the intention of its name.

"It looked like South Pittsburg was working its way back to the coveted position held, industrially speaking, some years ago. At that time, the 'Pittsburgh of the South,' so designated by the New Englanders who pioneered with iron furnaces long since silenced by the poor grade of ore mined at Inman in Marion County, was said to have had the largest payroll of any city of its size in the entire South."

A group of town merchants, businessmen, along with workmen from U.S. Stove and Marion Lumber, all pitched in money to come up with the $3,800 to buy the land.

In June, voters of South Pittsburg voted unanimously to approve a referendum for the city to issue $120,000 worth of bonds to build the plant. The project was put out to bid. That's when it came to a grinding halt.

All the builders in the area put in bids, which were higher than the amount the city could afford. The knitting mill project was on the verge of becoming a huge boondoggle. Marion Lumber Company was the only company willing and able to to build the facility for the price the city could afford.

As the president of Marion Lumber Company, S.L. Rogers saw the huge conflict of interest. How could he be mayor and take on this project using city funds? Perhaps some politicians wouldn't have cared. S.L. knew something had to go.

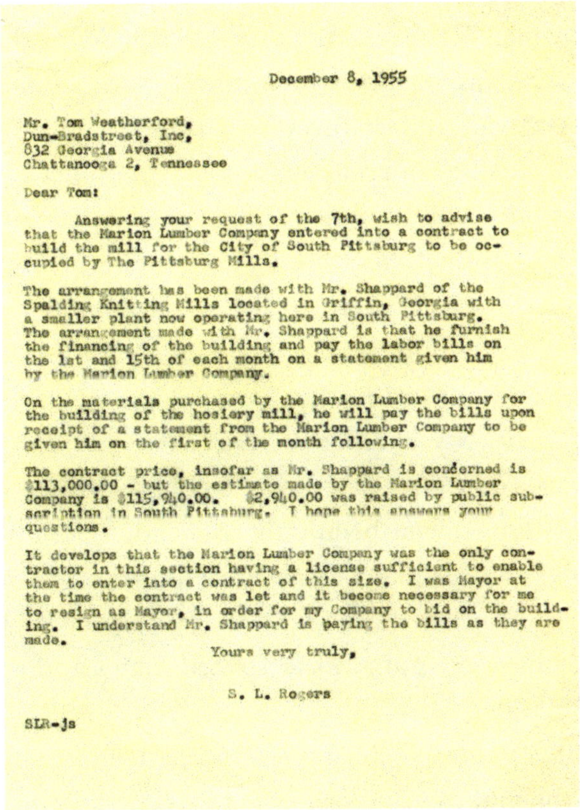

December 8, 1955

Mr. Tom Weatherford,
Dun-Bradstreet, Inc,
832 Georgia Avenue
Chattanooga 2, Tennessee

Dear Tom:

Answering your request of the 7th, wish to advise that the Marion Lumber Company entered into a contract to build the mill for the City of South Pittsburg to be occupied by The Pittsburg Mills.

The arrangement has been made with Mr. Shappard of the Spalding Knitting Mills located in Griffin, Georgia with a smaller plant now operating here in South Pittsburg. The arrangement made with Mr. Shappard is that he furnish the financing of the building and pay the labor bills on the 1st and 15th of each month on a statement given him by the Marion Lumber Company.

On the materials purchased by the Marion Lumber Company for the building of the hosiery mill, he will pay the bills upon receipt of a statement from the Marion Lumber Company to be given him on the first of the month following.

The contract price, insofar as Mr. Shappard is concerned is $113,000.00 - but the estimate made by the Marion Lumber Company is $115,940.00. $2,940.00 was raised by public subscription in South Pittsburg. I hope this answers your questions.

It develops that the Marion Lumber Company was the only contractor in this section having a license sufficient to enable them to enter into a contract of this size. I was Mayor at the time the contract was let and it become necessary for me to resign as Mayor, in order for my Company to bid on the building. I understand Mr. Shappard is paying the bills as they are made.

Yours very truly,

S. L. Rogers

SLR-js

*S.L. Rogers, Sr. retires as Mayor of South Pittsburg, T.N.*

In October 1955, Mayor S.L. Rogers, Sr. submitted his resignation. Lew Wilson Loyd became the new mayor.

Rogers wrote in his resignation letter: "The most difficult part of my decision has resulted from the knowledge that the wonderful relationship with you Commissioners is terminated, for I feel that the efforts of each member have resulted in an amazing amount of progress for our city in a very short time."

Meanwhile, S.L. kept the problem solving in the family. Bob Thomas was married to S.L. and Ruth's oldest daughter, Emmy. Bob ran and co-owned Marion Lumber Company and had started a concrete business on the side.

Bob wrote in his autobiography, "S.L. told me to go see Mr. Shapard and tell him that I would build the mill for him and he could pay me what he thought was fair."

The mill was built and opened in 1956. Writer David Head pointed out in his 2018 article for the *Marion County News* that the city avoided a huge financial disaster that would have come with an enormous bond debt for a factory that might have never been built. Instead, it became a place of employment for many local residents, mostly women, for more than 50 years. The socks that came out of that mill were sold in every state in the United States and across the world.

S.L. Rogers' many business interests often overlapped. Toward the end of his run at U.S. Stove, he became friendly with a young, new employee named John Hargis. About six months after Hargis started, he was set to get married. S.L. told him he had a house he and his new bride could rent. Sometime after that, Ruth Parham Rogers showed him one of their houses the Hargises could buy.

The new house came with a bonus job—helping to care for some of the Rogers cattle that grazed on the land next door. Hargis remembers an easy task that made for some pleasant encounters with one of the most powerful men in the region.

"I just watched after them and turned the water hose on in the trough," Hargis said. There never was any question when the big boss had come by to check in.

He had a '59 Ford car. He never drove a new car. This one was about five years old. He would just drive into the gate and push it open with the front of the car. He knew coming back, he would have to get out to open the gate, but going in, he just pushed it open. The sound announced his arrival, kinda like a big Southern doorbell."

Daughter Ruth backs up a story like this that talks about her father's choice of car and style of driving.

She says, "He had bought an old black Plymouth for me. He ended up getting me a beautiful new Ford instead and taking over the old car. He never bothered to look behind him when he was backing out of the parking space on Main Street. Everybody in town knew to watch for him, stop, and just let him back out. He was something else."

Hargis remembers S.L. Rogers being quite the presence

at U.S. Stove, as well. "He always smoked a big cigar. It didn't matter that this was the time that they were trying to get us to quit smoking. He could do whatever he wanted. We actually appreciated his cigar, because it always meant you could smell him coming. "Every morning when he came to work, he walked all the way through the plant to the back door, stood there, and peed at the back door into the yard."

Daughter Ruth confirms this habit, as well. "Papa would get behind a car or a tree and pee anywhere he needed to go. He was a country boy. This is just what country boys do."

## Ruth Parham's Challenges

*Stephen Leonard Rogers, Sr. & Ruth Parham Rogers*

Ruth Parham was a woman who left many questions behind. What did she do in Nashville in the years before she married? Why did she wait until she was 25 to marry a man fifteen years her senior?

Daughter Ruth suspects her mother simply had not met the right man as a very young woman. “She would have never been the type to get married simply for the sake of getting married.”

Instead, it appears Ruth headed to Nashville, where one of her brothers lived, and she got a job. Ruth also surmises that it was her Uncle Grady who knew Stephen Rogers from Chattanooga business and social circles. She says, “I think Grady decided his sister would be a good match for Stephen Rogers and set the whole thing up.”

In some ways, she was S.L. Rogers, Sr.'s rock, creating a home and producing the family he had always wanted. Daughter Ruth says her parents talked about everything, so she appears to have been her husband’s confidant and support, as well.

As her children grew, Ruth Parham took up real estate and showed care for folks outside her growing family. John Hargis was just a young U.S. Stove employee when he was interacting with both S.L. Sr. and Ruth.

“She sold me a house. Of course, I had no money, and she said you don’t need no money. She said you just meet your wife and meet me down at the lawyer’s office. And I went into the lawyer’s office and probably didn’t have $3 in my pocket. And she sold me a house and wrote everything down on tablet paper. She wrote down everything, you know, how much I paid each month on interest. I still remember that just as well, but I had it all listed on tablet paper. I wished I had kept it, but I didn't.

"She was like family to us. When my first child passed away, she was one of the first there at my house, bringing food. She was just a great support to us. And it was just amazing during the time my son, Gerald, was born; she would come to my house all the time, and in the later years, she got so that she couldn't see very well. She would park in the yard and have me drive her home if it got late. "

Ruth's grandchildren say she was as big an influence on their lives as their grandfather was. Amy Turner Burns says, "There's no forgetting our grandmother. She taught us all our manners. She taught us how to act. She had us over to play every Sunday. She'd let us dress up in her clothes. She had these little mink stoles that went around with these little fox clips. She'd make us little parties at her house and make lunch so that she could show us how to use all the right utensils."

Amy's sister, Nancy Anne "Roo" Turner Hookey, says, "I know people laugh at me today because I eat so slowly. But it was my grandmother who told me every bite I should chew at least twenty times. I don't still count, but I know that she's the one who instilled that in me. She's the reason I'm a slow eater."

Amy also remembers Ruth's fascination with cemeteries. "She'd load us up and take us in the car to these places in the country. She'd walk us through explaining who different family members were, as we passed by their graves. Family history was very important to her."

While Ruth was clearly a devoted wife, mother and grandmother, there were also clear challenges, though there weren't the same labels and names early in the 20th century. Ruth Rogers Wainwright believes her mother was bipolar, beginning in her 40s.

Ruth talks about how intelligent her mother was, how in a different generation she could have had a thriving career of her own, perhaps in real estate.

By her 40s, Ruth Parham Rogers was having challenges. "My sisters said Mama changed in her 40s. I wouldn't know, but as I knew her, looking back, she would go through relatively long periods of being happy and cheerful followed by relatively long periods of being sad, but she functioned well all the time and never took to bed or seemed too detached at any time. I think my father was her stabilizing influence. After he died, her depression was awful for the remainder of her life.

"My mother would get up in the middle of the night and start rearranging furniture. And my dad just let her do it. She could also get very depressed, and we all kind of chuckled about it because we didn't know what it was. It saddens me deeply that we didn't know what it was because of the agony that she had to go through with that. But we would laugh and say, 'If Mama was in a good mood, everybody would get Christmas presents. If Mama was not in a good mood, nobody got any Christmas presents, and that was true of many Christmases. And she was never treated for it in any way, she was never hospitalized with it in any way."

Daughter Ruth is very open in talking about not only her mother's mental health challenges, but her own, as well. "I was diagnosed as bipolar in my 30s, but I think I have learned in therapy that I was having challenges as early as age ten. I had a deep depression then for seemingly no reason and told no one. I pretended I was OK for about a week. I remember other bouts of depression as well in my teens and twenties, always gritting my teeth, acting normal, and telling no one."

Ruth is not the only descendent of S.L. Rogers, Sr. and Ruth Parham Rogers, who has faced mental health challenges. There are many examples in every branch of the family of all four Rogers children. There have been decades to look for a common thread. Many, including Ruth, believe the affliction came through their mother's side of the family. "I think that's the source, because I don't think it was our father. He was just steady as a rock. He didn't show any signs of it."

The trait carried on through the generations, through all of SLR, Sr.'s and Ruth's children, and their children and grandchildren.

Richard Rogers said he accepts this as part of the family story. "I'm not ashamed of it at all. I recognize it, and it's just something that is a genetic disposition for mental illness. And over the years, I've given quite a bit of support to mental illness in a lot of different ways, and I intend to continue to do so in the future.

My little brother Bill had it. I think that my youngest older sister had it. I think my dad had it, but just didn't want to admit it. Deep down, I think he knew. Then my son, my oldest son, August's older sister, I mean, I can name them on and on and on, and it's, you know, it's just the reality of the situation."

It's not so simple to say some members of the family have had mental health challenges. Many of those same relatives were blessed with incredible intelligence and talent.

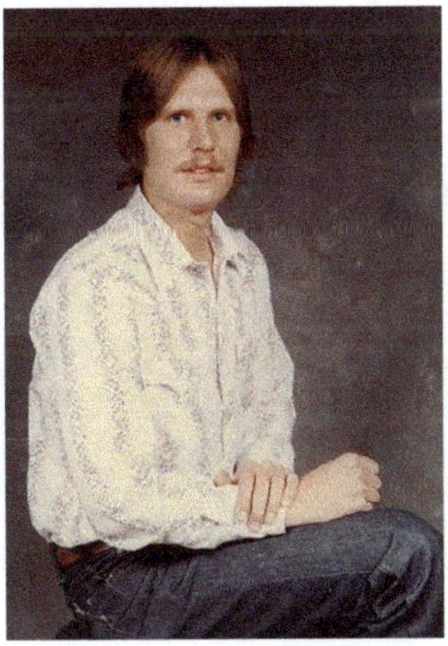

*William "Bill" Forrester Rogers, August 13, 1955-November 11, 2012*

Richard and Steve Rogers' youngest brother, Bill, was a talented poet who wrote a number of books of poetry.

Steve shares one of his favorite poems. His brother wrote this one six months before he passed away in 2012.

## Dollar

*Empty pocket*
*Filled with change,*
*Please don't stop it.*
*Not too strange.*

*Break a dollar*
*Not a heart.*
*Rich forever,*
*Just a start.*

*Cash in hand*
*On the street,*
*Understand*
*With your feet.*

William F. Rogers
May 31, 2012

Great-granddaughter Stephanie Rogers Esper, Steve's daughter, picked up on the legacy of mental health challenges in her genealogy research. "During the genealogy work, I called my dad, because I said, 'Dad where did this come from? Because where I see that it possibly came from was Ruth Parham Rogers.' And he agreed that that's where he thought it originated. Because he said that you never knew what kind of mindset she was going to have, what you were going to get."

## Golf Course and Bowling Alley

Grandson Reece Thomas points out how civic minded his grandfather was. "If he thought the town needed something, and he had the means to do it, he'd build it. He built the Knitting Mill building, because he knew we needed some industry. That was the same inspiration when it came time to build a golf course, because he knew the businesspeople of South Pittsburg needed a place to meet, socialize, and interact. As a result of that, the whole town shut down every Thursday afternoon and went and played golf."

Daughter Ruth remembered her brother, Leonard, coming home from the University of Tennessee, where he learned how to play golf. This inspired SLR, Sr. to learn how to play, too. He instantly fell in love with the game. Ruth remembered her father declaring, "'We need a golf course here!' So, he bought this farm out on Sweetens Cove Road.

We went out there, and it was just a plowed-up field. Papa said, 'You get to hit the first golf ball here.' So, he pulled out a golf ball, and I hit it. And then he hit one, and you know, that was the beginning of that.

"It really was the beginning of something huge. What started as a fun civic project by 2019 had been named one of the top 50 best 9-hole golf courses in the world. It attracted the likes of NFL Hall of Fame quarterback Peyton Manning and world-ranked tennis player Andy Roddick. They are a group that invested in the course and are turning it into a top golfing destination.

"S.L. also made baseball an official part of the South Pittsburg community. 94-year-old Brad Carter remembers getting hired to work at the foundry as a teenager in 1946. He says, "In the late 40s, or about 1950, Mr. Rogers built a baseball field right next to the U.S. Stove Company foundry, right near Paul Turner's food market. The first game that was ever played there, Lenny Rogers was the starting pitcher, and I was the catcher.

"I played baseball on that field for the next four years. Every Sunday, Mr. Rogers would be in the window at U.S. Stove watching every amateur baseball game we played there."

# Grandfather

*SL Rogers, III, Reece Thomas, SL Rogers, Sr, Carolyn Rogers, Ruth Rogers & Julia W. Rogers.*

While the world of South Pittsburg knew S.L. Rogers as a civic leader and captain of industry, to most of his descendants alive in 2020, his legacy was as their grandfather or "Papa."

To grandson, Richard Rogers, he planted the seed of a budding businessman.

"He gave me a cigar box and said, 'Richard, here's this cigar box. It is something you need to take. And as you grow older when you save money, save it in this cigar box and remember that if you'll save that money in this cigar box, then it'll grow—and it'll grow. Remember, you don't go into debt. Don't buy anything unless you have the money to buy it to begin with.' So, he gave me that cigar box.

I got a paper route here in South Pittsburg, and I had 120 customers. I delivered papers on my bicycle on weekends and after school every day. I made $30 every two months, and I got paid in quarters. So, every time I got four quarters, I would tape them together for one dollar and put them in the cigar box. I had a secret hiding place in the attic. This was a special place in a dark corner where none of my siblings could squeeze into. This was crucial because I had four brothers and sisters.

I felt safe keeping it there. I finally got 100 rolls of four quarters to make $100. I went to the bank and got a $100 bill. I walked around feeling so rich. And I thought, 'You know, I liked getting that first one so much, I think I'm going to go for the second one!' And so, the influence that he had with that cigar box has been something that I remembered for many, many years."

It wasn't just the money lesson. It was the ability that S.L.R, Sr., this powerful politician and businessman, had to make each one of his grandchildren feel special.

He loved golf and loved to bowl.

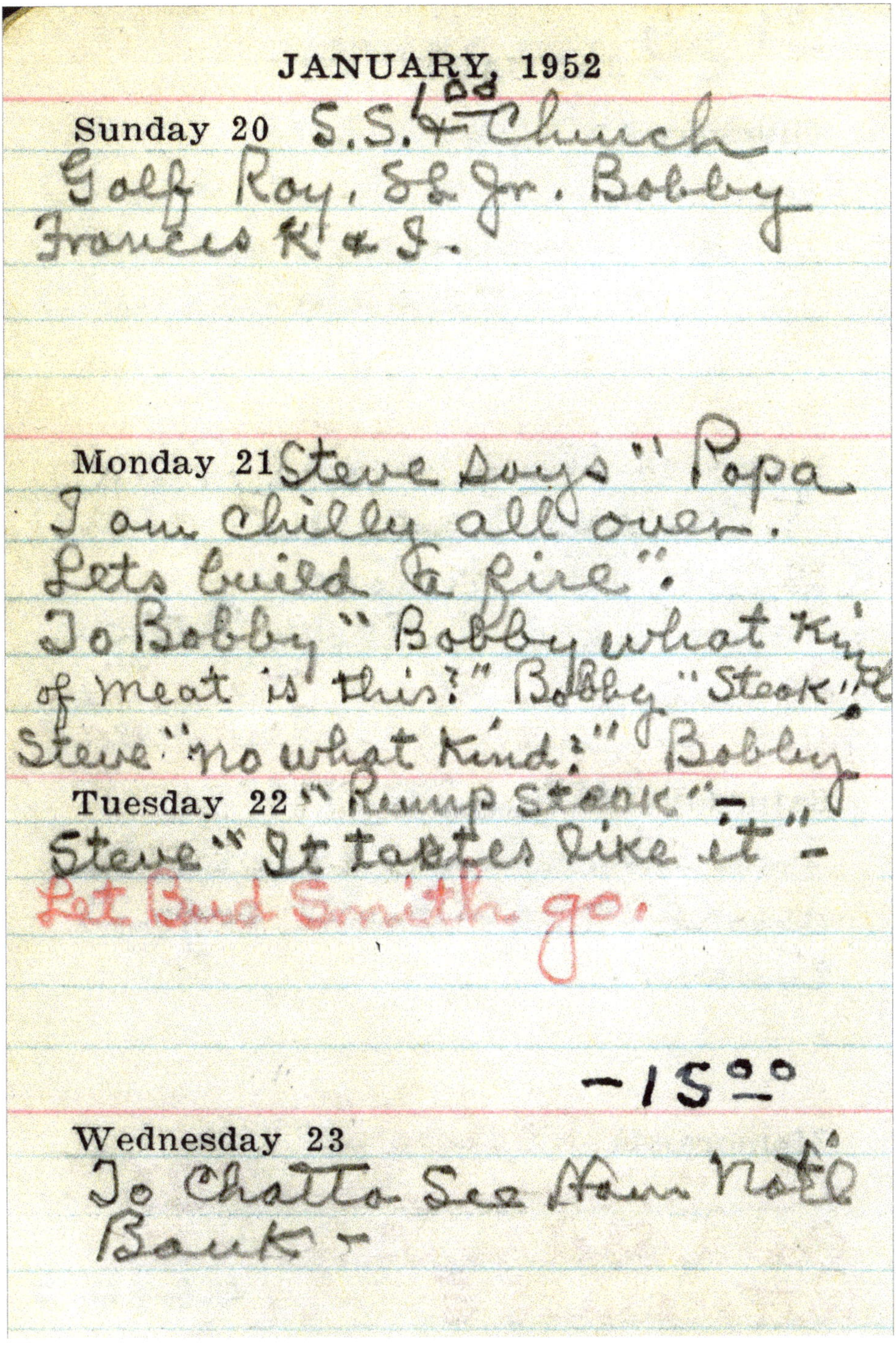

JANUARY, 1952

Sunday 20 S.S. & Church
Golf Roy, S.L. Jr. Bobby
Frances K. & S.

Monday 21 Steve says "Popa
I am chilly all over.
Lets build a fire".
To Bobby "Bobby what kind
of meat is this?" Bobby "Steak".
Steve "no what kind?" Bobby

Tuesday 22 "Rump steak" —
Steve "It tastes like it" —
Let Bud Smith go.

—15.00

Wednesday 23
To Chatta See Ham Natl
Bank —

*S.L.R. Sr. saves a memory with oldest grandchild, Steve.*

His oldest grandson Steve remembers some classic Saturday afternoon spent with his grandfather at the bowling alley.

"Papa never got excited—that was one of his strengths in my opinion—the ability to remain calm.

When I was about fourteen, I played in the Saturday morning league at Junction Lanes in Kimball. Papa would either come to the bowling alley and bowl with us boys all afternoon or bring us back to the lanes if we went home first, either way paying for all our games.

One Saturday we went home from the league bowling, and he picked us up around noon to go back and bowl in the afternoon.

He never could drive too well. He was older, and his driving abilities were getting even worse. We came to a stop sign at Dixie Lee junction in Kimball, not far from the lanes. Apparently, Papa hit the gas instead of the brake ramming into the car in front of him, which caused that car to hit the car in front of it. It was a three-car pile-up!

Papa got out and talked to the two drivers whose cars he had damaged. He found out he was related to both of them in some way. That actually wasn't that uncommon for Marion County in the early 1960s.

Instead of waiting for the police to arrive, he went to his trunk, opened it, and got out his bowling ball. He then said to us, 'Boys, come on—we're going bowling.'

He told the people whose cars were damaged that when

the police arrived, he would be at the bowling alley. We then left the scene and the damaged cars sitting in the road and walked to the bowling alley and got us a lane. We put on our shoes and began bowling, as if nothing bad had happened.

After a few frames, the police did, in fact, arrive. They made out the accident report between frames and left.

After we finished, we came out of the bowling alley to find the police had moved Papa's damaged car. Turns out it was still drivable. So, we got in, and he drove us home; never once missing a beat or getting upset about the situation.

He had intended to take us boys bowling on a Saturday afternoon, and that's exactly what he did.

Betty Turner Kane is the daughter of middle daughter Nancy Jane. She remembers golf lessons from her grandfather.

"I remember he would sit on the golf cart and then watch me. I would try to hit the ball as hard as I could and of course miss it or top it or whatever. He would say, 'You know, OK. Let's go again.'

I would do it and miss again. Then he says, 'Betty I've got an idea. All I want is for you to just look straight at that ball on the tee from the back of your swing all the way through. I'm going to watch the ball, and then I'll tell you where it went.'

I was able to start hitting the ball that way, and I developed a pretty long drive. In fact, when I started practicing law and playing golf with other attorneys, they'd always want to be paired with me for Round Robin games, because we could play from my drives. It was Papa who got me started with that."

The attention that both Papa and Mama Ruth showered on the grandchildren and the home they had at Magnolia and 4th, "The Big House", made for a natural pool of playmates.

Amy Turner Burns, daughter of Nancy Jane Rogers, says, "For the first twenty years of my life, life with the family was all we needed. We didn't need any other friends. We had five kids in our family; Emmy had three boys, Leonard had five children. All of us first cousins were family and friends. We played together every day. Our grandparents were the driving force of the family, creating a lot of time to spend time together."

Grandson Reece Thomas, son of Emmy Rogers Thomas and Bob Thomas, agrees. He says, "We rode bicycles all over town. A.J. Gudgers was a little store up here on Second Street, and Papa lived in the 300 block of Magnolia. We'd always have to ride by his house to get to the store to buy candy. He was always sitting there with a top hat on and usually smoking a cigar. You would go in, and he'd sort of give you a hug from his chair. Then, he'd reach over with his right hand and pull out this old cigar box full of change, and he'd hand us all change. We'd say, 'Hello. We love you!' and take off to the candy store."

Their grandfather's funeral was a huge shock to the

grandchildren. Of course, there was the grief in losing their beloved Papa. Beyond that, the children were shocked to learn that this special man they only thought of as belonging to them, actually was a huge presence in South Pittsburg.

Reece remembers, "My mother, Emmy, and Amy's mother, Nancy, came to school and called us all out of classes. I looked around, and there were eleven of us first cousins. There was somebody in every one of those eight grades. They told us Papa had died.

They had the viewing with Papa's casket at their house. The line of people who came to pay their respects went on for hours and hours. As we went to the service at Cumberland Presbyterian, we had to fight our way through the crowd of people who had shown up. People were standing out in the yard just to be at the service."

Richard remembers, "A lot of people were talking about how he had loaned them or given them money, and I think the majority of them never paid him back, but he didn't care. He was just that kind of guy."

S.L. Rogers, Sr. was also the kind of man who passed his good fortune and hard work onto the next generation. Daughter Ruth explains how he left a legacy and opportunity for each of his adult children and their descendants. "Leonard had controlling stock in the Stove Company. For Emmy, there was controlling stock in the Lumber Company, and for her and her husband, Bobby. For Nancy and Paul, there was the grocery store that he planned and gave to them. It was called, 'Paul's Food Market.'

And for me, there was some stock in the Stove Company and some stock in the Lumber Company. I had nothing out of the supermarket. I got less than everybody else, but I think I made good with it. The bulk of it was from the Stove Company. I divided that in three. That money sent both of our daughters through college. And it sent us on some family trips. I knew all along that he cared."

You can find milestones of all these businesses by milling through old local newspapers.

*The South Pittsburg Hustler* announced Paul Turner's taking over of a local grocery store in 1950. "An important business transaction was consummated this week when Paul Turner took over the stock and good will of the Ambrose Cash Market at Fourth Street and Cedar Avenue, where the new owner will continue the business under the name of Paul's Food Market. Mr. Turner has been connected with the Great Atlantic and Pacific Tea Co. since 1939 except for three years' service to Uncle Sam during World War II, and manager of the local store since 1946. He is a sterling young man of worth and is well trained in the mercantile business."

The opening of the store at a bigger location made for a funny headline in 1958. "Paul's Supermarket Opening Big Success...but mighty hard on the chickens."

The article explains, "Paul's Supermarket owned and operated by Paul W. Turner, located at the corner of Cedar Avenue and Fifth Street; had a successful opening last weekend in one of the most attractive and convenient food markets in the Valley. According to John D. Mayfield, in charge of Paul's meat department, the market sold over 600 Swift Premium frying chickens over Friday and Saturday and could have sold over 200 more had they been available. Statistic-wise, according to the latest figures released by the Chamber of Commerce, this represents a choice piece of fried chicken for every resident in South Pittsburg with seconds for about 600 of those with more demanding appetites."

Such an event most likely would have made it into one of the numerous diaries that S.L. Rogers, Sr. kept throughout his life. The small little books contain minute details from his daily life. Yet, they paint a picture of a life that was lived with thought and intention. That drive has continued to provide an example and inspiration to the generations that have followed.

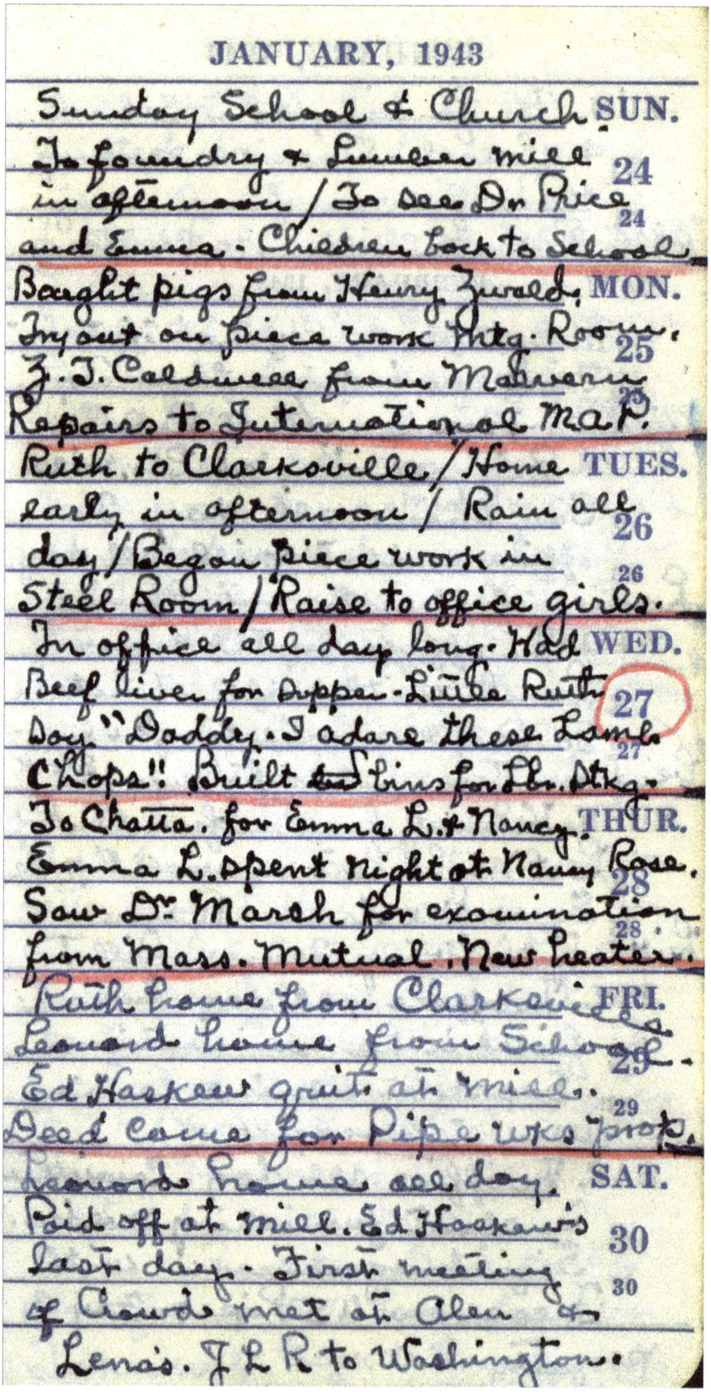
JANUARY, 1943

SUN. 24
Sunday School & Church.
To foundry & Lumber mill
in afternoon / To see Dr Price
and Emma - Children back to School.

MON. 25
Bought pigs from Henry Zwald.
Try out on piece work Mtg. Room.
Z. T. Caldwell from Malvern
Repairs to International M&P.

TUES. 26
Ruth to Clarksville / Home
early in afternoon / Rain all
day / Began piece work in
Steel Room / Raise to office girls.

WED. 27
In office all day long. Had
Beef liver for supper - Little Ruth
say "Daddy, I adore these Lamb
Chops!" Built bins for Lbr. Stkg.

THUR. 28
To Chatta. for Emma L. & Nancy.
Emma L. spent night at Nancy Rose.
Saw Dr. March for examination
from Mass. Mutual. New heater.

FRI. 29
Ruth home from Clarksville.
Leonard home from School.
Ed Haskew quits at mill.
Deed came for Pipe wks prop.

SAT. 30
Leonard home all day.
Paid off at mill. Ed Haskew's
last day. First meeting
of Crowd met at Alan &
Lena's. FLR to Washington.

*S.L. Rogers, Sr. captures important moments from his business day and precious moment with daughter, "Little Ruth."*

Great-grandson Russ Rogers knows they inspired his own father, Richard. "My dad had his grandfather's diaries. He has tried to replicate his ethics and morals. I will always remember my dad trying to become like my great-grandfather, because he looked up to him so much."

The diaries show a man who is meticulous in his business dealings while also being a devoted family man.

## A Life Well-Lived

Daughter Ruth has carried a special memory of life with Papa through her entire life. "Whenever we went somewhere in the car for any length of time or any time of day, my father would begin to sing. For example, a trip to Chattanooga took at least an hour, even longer than that on Route 41, which only had two lanes. Our father would start singing, and then we would all sing together. None of us had an incredible voice, but we could all carry a tune and harmonize from time to time. 'There's a Long, Long Trail a Winding into the Land of My Dreams' I recall as a favorite.

From singing to caring for us, he was a benevolent patriarch. An important mission in his life was to take care of his family, financially and in their well-being. He deeply loved every one of us, and his grandchildren were the lights of his life. His desire for heirs was generously fulfilled with the births of SLR III, Richard, and Bill. He, Mother and I, as well as others, crowded into Steve's small nursery and watched him sleep for as long as we were allowed! Of course, he loved all the girls as well!

SLR, Sr. was always a faithful churchgoer and was active in the church as a church officer, serving as deacon and elder over the years. Sometime around his late 70s or 80, I noticed that he was reading the Bible quite often, which I had never noticed him doing before. Once he asked me what I thought about one of the judgment passages (not that I knew anything much about the Bible at that time). In retrospect, I have wondered if he had done something in his life that he considered terribly sinful and was fearful about judgment after his death.

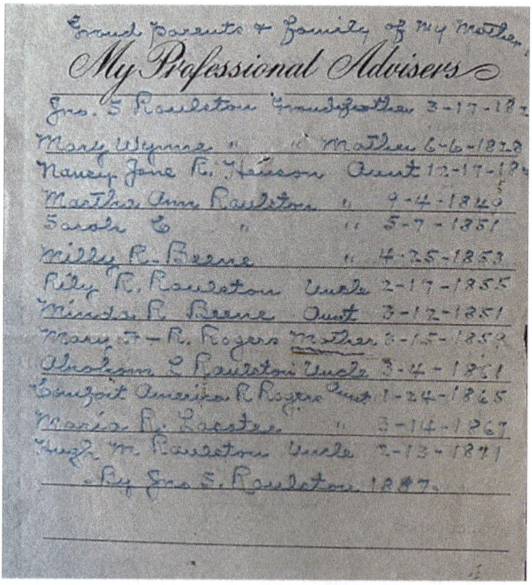
Grand parents & family of my mother
My Professional Advisers
Jno. S Roulston Grandfather 3-17-18
Mary Wynne " " Mother 6-6-1828
Nancy Jane R. Henson Aunt 12-17-18
Martha Ann Roulston " 9-4-1849
Sarah E " " 5-7-1851
Milly R. Beene " 4-25-1853
Riley R. Roulston Uncle 2-17-1855
Minda R. Beene Aunt 3-12-1851
Mary F. R. Rogers Mother 8-15-1859
Abraham L. Roulston Uncle 3-4-1861
Comfort America R. Rogers Aunt 1-24-1865
Maria R. Lacaster " 3-14-1867
Hugh M. Roulston Uncle 2-13-1871
By Jno. S. Roulston 1887.

*S.L.R., Sr. works on his family ancestry in one of his daily diaries.*

At the end of his life, he was bedridden for about three months, dying at home from congestive heart failure. I was in graduate school at Vanderbilt and came home every weekend. He had some dementia, but we would talk about various things when I was with him. He would lament that he couldn't do anything, couldn't take care of anything. I assured him that he had always taken care of all of us, and now it was our turn to take care of him. He smiled, and I think it made him feel better. I was among a few of our family members who were with him when he breathed his last breath. He died March 24, 1965, the day after my 26th birthday.

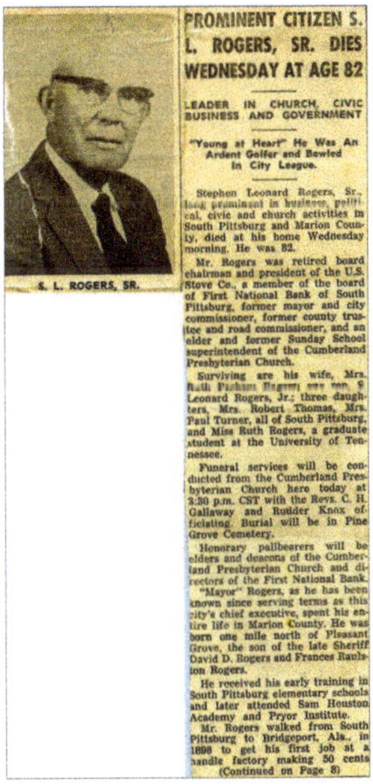

S. L. ROGERS, SR.

PROMINENT CITIZEN S. L. ROGERS, SR. DIES WEDNESDAY AT AGE 82

LEADER IN CHURCH, CIVIC BUSINESS AND GOVERNMENT

"Young at Heart" He Was An Ardent Golfer and Bowled In City League.

Stephen Leonard Rogers, Sr., long prominent in business, political, civic and church activities in South Pittsburg and Marion County, died at his home Wednesday morning. He was 82.

Mr. Rogers was retired board chairman and president of the U.S. Stove Co., a member of the board of First National Bank of South Pittsburg, former mayor and city commissioner, former county trustee and road commissioner, and an elder and former Sunday School superintendent of the Cumberland Presbyterian Church.

Surviving are his wife, Mrs. [illegible] Leonard Rogers, Jr.; three daughters, Mrs. Robert Thomas, Mrs. Paul Turner, all of South Pittsburg, and Miss Ruth Rogers, a graduate student at the University of Tennessee.

Funeral services will be conducted from the Cumberland Presbyterian Church here today at 3:30 p.m. CST with the Revs. C. H. Gallaway and Rudder Knox officiating. Burial will be in Pine Grove Cemetery.

Honorary pallbearers will be elders and deacons of the Cumberland Presbyterian Church and directors of the First National Bank.

"Mayor" Rogers, as he has been known since serving terms as this city's chief executive, spent his entire life in Marion County. He was born one mile north of Pleasant Grove, the son of the late Sheriff David D. Rogers and Frances Raulston Rogers.

He received his early training in South Pittsburg elementary schools and later attended Sam Houston Academy and Pryor Institute.

Mr. Rogers walked from South Pittsburg to Bridgeport, Ala., in 1898 to get his first job at a handle factory making 50 cents

(Continued on Page 8)

*Stephen Leonard Rogers, Sr.'s Obituary*

After his death, things began to fall apart. The family had so many challenges. There was the manifestation of bi-polar disorder, along with alcoholism, especially in Leonard, Jr. We didn't completely come apart, but things certainly changed. I was there only on occasional weeklong trips during the year after Papa passed."

# 4

# A SON'S LEGACY

## The Job SLR Rogers, Junior Was Born Into

No one probably ever asked Stephen Leonard Rogers, Jr. what he wanted to be when he grew up. There was no need for such a discussion. He was born with a purpose—to take over U.S. Stove Company.

Perhaps, if someone would have asked Lenny Rogers what he really wanted to be, if he wanted to use his considerable talent as a writer and a poet, then his story would have ended differently.

*Stephen Leonard Rogers, Jr.; McCallie School.*

His oldest daughter, Julia, remembers his artistic side. "He used to draw pictures, portraits of us. I have some portraits that he's drawn of us that are just little pencil sketches."

S.L. Rogers, Jr.'s life as a bohemian artist was never a consideration.

Stephen Rogers III is the oldest son. He believes his father had no choice as to what his father's future would hold. "I think he was put in a box, and that box was to run that company, and that was in his mind that it was what he was expected to do. I don't think it made him happy. I mean, he did what he had to because he was very smart. He had a very high IQ. But running the company didn't really lend itself to what his passion was. He was more of an artsy kind of person, a poet and left-brained inclined. He loved handwriting analysis stuff and writing. He didn't care about balance sheets and profit and loss statements."

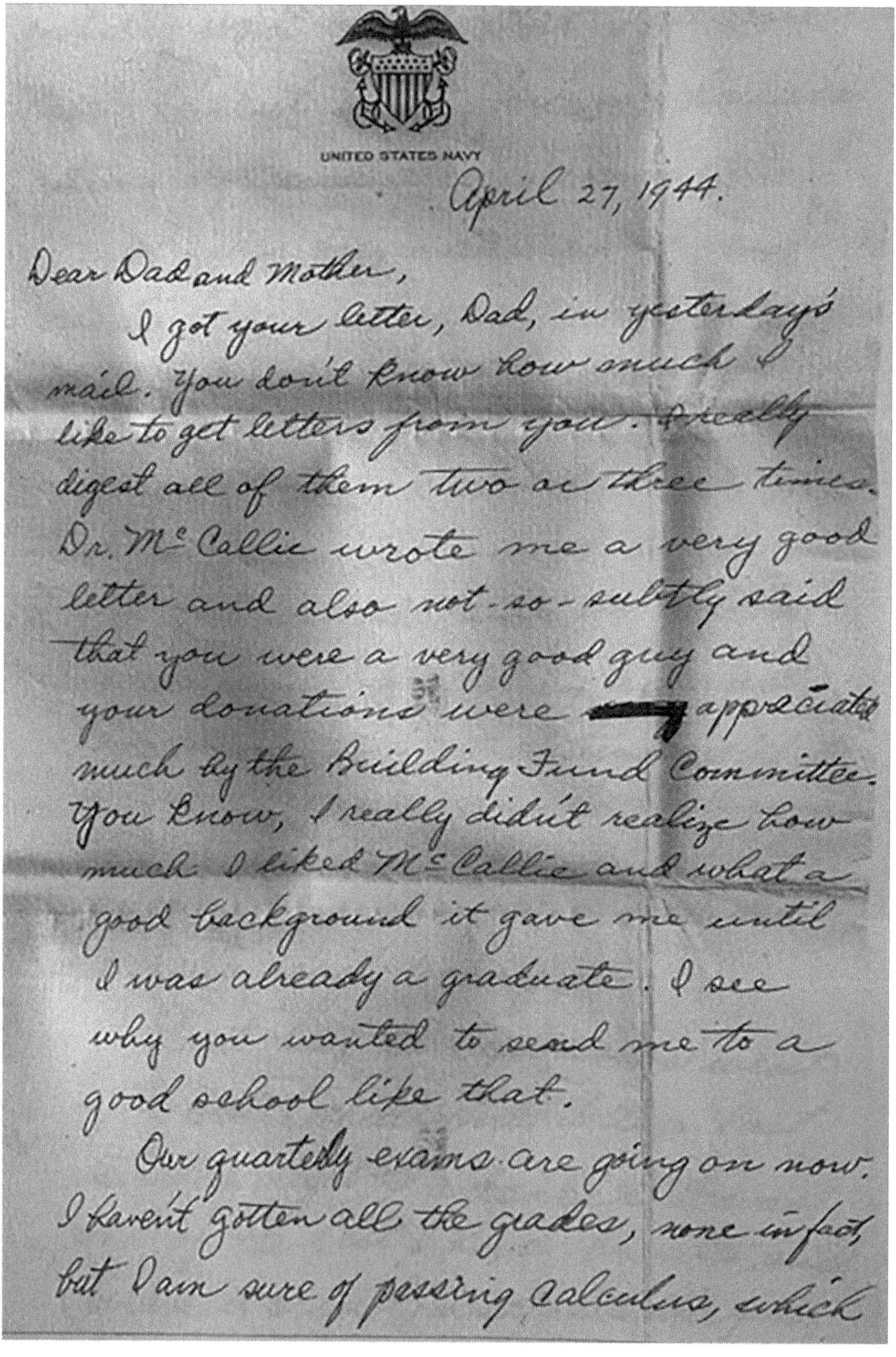

UNITED STATES NAVY

April 27, 1944.

Dear Dad and Mother,

I got your letter, Dad, in yesterday's mail. You don't know how much I like to get letters from you. I really digest all of them two or three times. Dr. McCallie wrote me a very good letter and also not-so-subtly said that you were a very good guy and your donations were [redacted] appreciated much by the Building Fund Committee. You know, I really didn't realize how much I liked McCallie and what a good background it gave me until I was already a graduate. I see why you wanted to send me to a good school like that.

Our quarterly exams are going on now. I haven't gotten all the grades, none in fact, but I am sure of passing Calculus, which

*Leonard Rogers writes a letter home to his parents while attending the Webb School of Architecture.*

His niece Betty Turner Kane remembered that as a girl, she thought her Uncle Leonard was the smartest person she'd ever met. "He knew about philosophers and things like that. My own father and his family had grown up during the depression and weren't particularly well educated. They were never interested in reading novels, discussing Plato, or things like that, but Uncle Leonard and I would have conversations that no one else in my family was interested in having."

S. L. ROGERS RETIRES AFTER 25 YEARS IN THE STOVE MFG. BUSINESS

ENTIRE LIFE AND BUSINESS INTERESTS SPENT IN VALLEY

J. Leonard Raulston, Elected Chm. of Board—S. L. Rogers, Jr. is President.

S. L. ROGERS, SR. Retired

J. LEONARD RAULSTON Chmn. of the Board

S. L. ROGERS, JR. President

S. L. Rogers, Sr., who has been board chairman and president of the United States Stove Company for the past 25 years, announced his retirement from active management of the company Tuesday, February 20, at a meeting of the board of directors. His resignation was accepted and the board elected J. Leonard Raulston as chairman of the board of directors, with S. L. Rogers, Jr. as president.

Mr. Raulston and Mr. Rogers, Jr., have both been active as executives of the company for a considerable length of time, and according to a joint statement by them, U. S. Stove Company will continue to follow past policies of operation.

J. Leonard Raulston is a graduate of the University of Tennessee. He was a member of the UT faculty for a number of years prior to joining the stove company in 1937. He steps up to chairman of the board from the office of vice president and general manager.

For two years president of American Institute of Appliance Manufacturers, 1957-58, he was chosen the American speaker to the International Institute of Appliance Manufacturers meeting in Brussels, traveling under the authority of the State Department.

Raulston is presently serving on the Board of Trustees of the University of Tennessee. As chairman of the Marion County Industrial Committee he has been an influencial figure in attracting industrial prospects to the valley. He is past president of the Rotary Club and was this year, during his absence from the city, elected president of the Chamber of Commerce. This office he was forced to turn down due to company business keeping him away from the city much of the year. He is co-owner of Raulston-Pryor Quarry near Bennett's Lake on the Tennessee river.

Married to the former Miss Agnes Hicks, the Raulstons have two sons, Leonard, Jr. and Michael. They are members of Christ Episcopal Church.

S. L. Rogers, Jr., is also a graduate of the University of Tennessee, the class of '49. He is married to the former Miss Ann Forrester of Union City and they have a family of two daughters, Carolyn, Julia; and three sons, Steve, Richard and Bill.

Rogers came to U. S. Stove Company from UT, working in the foundry for some time before accepting his executive responsibilities as a vice president. He has served the Junior Chamber of Commerce as president and is a charter member of the Rotary Club, of which he is the incoming vice president.

He is the founderer and president of Pyrmid Box Company of Cleveland, Tennessee.

The Rogers are members of the Cumberland Presbyterian Church where S. L., Jr. serves on the board of deacons and as Sunday School superintendent.

S. L. ROGERS, SR. RETIRES

After 25 years in the harness as

(Continued on page 6)

*Stephen Leonard Rogers, Sr. retires*

"Lenny" Rogers was taking over a company that his father had spent the second half of his life raising from the ashes. Under his father's leadership, U.S. Stove Company had gone from nothing to one of the top companies of its kind in the country.

Rodger Castleberry points out, "When SLR, Sr. stepped down, there were twenty manufacturers of similar equipment. Wood and coal heaters, fireplaces, kitchen ranges, kerosene cook stoves and heaters, and a small operation making cast iron lawn furniture. They were also making gas appliances, and they had bought Lawson manufacturing of Cincinnati, Ohio, where they manufactured furnaces and room heaters. U.S. Stove was the fourth largest company of its kind in the country, so it wasn't the biggest, but it was the only one so diversified."

Son Richard believes his father felt the high expectations from Day One. "I think he felt a tremendous amount of pressure, particularly because of the things that my grandfather had accomplished during his lifetime."

# The Good Years: Married

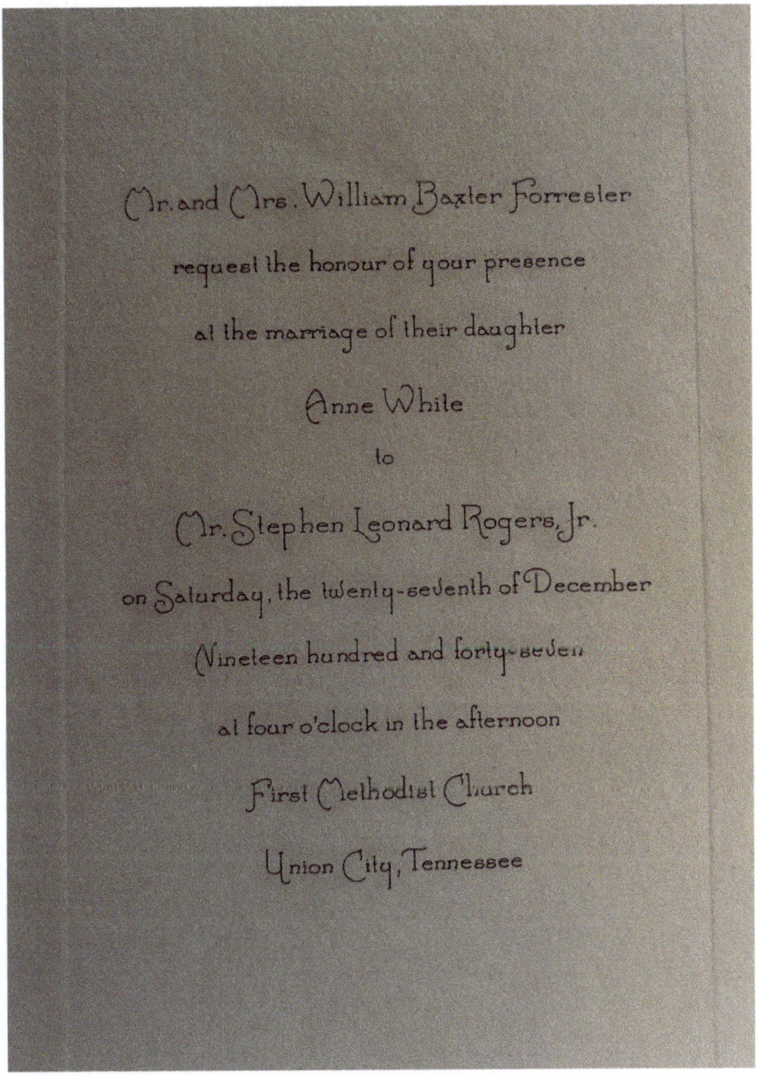

Mr. and Mrs. William Baxter Forrester

request the honour of your presence

at the marriage of their daughter

Anne White

to

Mr. Stephen Leonard Rogers, Jr.

on Saturday, the twenty-seventh of December

Nineteen hundred and forty-seven

at four o'clock in the afternoon

First Methodist Church

Union City, Tennessee

*Anne White Forrester & Stephen Leonard Rogers, Jr.'s Wedding Announcement, 1947.*

Even with little to no choice in his career, Lenny Rogers found happiness in his young adult life. He found his partner in fellow college student, Anne White Forrester.

*Anne Forrester marries S.L. Rogers, Jr. 1947.*

By 1955, they had five children, three boys and two girls. And by many accounts, the young couple was popular and active on the social scene.

*Mother & Son: Anne Forrester Rogers & Stephen Leonard Rogers, III*

*The five Rogers siblings, L to R: Richard, Julie, Bill, Carolyn and Steve.*

He oversaw a business that held steady through the 60s. Old balance sheets show that Sears Roebuck was the main customer. The profits and losses of the company didn't change much. There wasn't a lot of growth. The company held steady making a reasonable profit each year.

*Three generations: Stephen Leonard Rogers, III, SL Rogers, Sr. & SL Rogers Jr.*

At work, Lenny was connected to the most powerful businesspeople in southern Tennessee while still having time and interest in developing his employees.

John Hargis has fond memories of working for Leonard Rogers. "He took me on my first trip. I came from a poor family. I had never been out of the area. But Leonard bought a company up in Pennsylvania and insisted that I needed to come with him to check it out.

I didn't have any of the right clothes to go to a cold place like Pennsylvania in the wintertime. When we ran into six feet of snow, Leonard had to buy me clothes. He must have really seen something in me to give me opportunities like that. He's also the one who started moving me up through the company. I was only in my 20s, and they moved me into supervision.

He simply was one of the best people I ever worked for. He was very generous and had a great sense of humor. He had these red pants he liked to wear. Seemed like he wore them every day. Every morning, we would meet up, and he would buy me a cup of coffee. And every morning, I would tease him about his red pants. He'd say, 'I'm just trying to wear these S.O.B.'s out.'"

Leonard also had a very outgoing personality and many friends, including his brother-in-law, Bobby Thomas, who was married to Leonard's sister, Emmy. Son Richard shares a funny story that his Uncle Bobby told him many times over the years.

"It was a warm summer day, and my father and Bob Thomas were playing golf somewhere down in Alabama. They were very competitive with each other. They were both club champions at the Sweetens Cove Golf Course near South Pittsburg, the course that my grandfather built and donated in 1952.

They had a wager on that game they played that day in Alabama. Bob came out the winner, winning $17 from my dad.

After the golf match, they rode home together back to South Pittsburg. My dad was driving as they went through several small towns in Alabama. In one particular small town, the speed limit dropped to 30 mph as my dad was going 50 mph.

A patrolman pulled them over and proceeded to give my dad a speeding ticket. The officer explained the way it worked in this small town. My dad would have to come to the town hall right away and pay for the ticket.

Bob and Dad went there, and Bob stayed in the car while my dad went in to pay the fine. Bob waited and waited for a very long time. It was actually getting dark by this time. He finally decided he better go in and see what was going on.

When Bob went inside, he found Dad sitting in a small room with a single light bulb swinging from the ceiling. My father and a city official were arguing about something. Bob asked what the problem was.

The city official said, "I am telling Mr. Rogers that the

fine needs to be paid before you gentlemen are free to go. The fine is $35, but he keeps insisting that the fine should actually be $52 since he was going 52 mph. He also says he only has $35, but gentlemen you will remain here until you can get the full $52 amount."

My dad looked at Bob with a grin and said, "Well, I guess we will be here until we can come up with $17."

I am sure you can figure out the rest of this story.

My dad got his $17 loss back from Bob!

## Taking On More Responsibility

**S.L. Rogers Jr. Elected Board Chairman at U.S. Stove**

**OFFICERS OF U.S. STOVE**—United States Stove Co. of South Pittsburg has announced some recent executive changes. Officers of the firm who are pictured are, from left, L. Morris Haynie, treasurer; Michael J. Herschel, vice president, sales; S.L. Rogers Jr., president and chairman of the board; S.L. Rogers III, assistant secretary-treasurer, and John B. Roper, vice president, manufacturing.

S.L. Rogers Jr., president of United States Stove Co. of South Pittsburg since 1962, was recently elected to chairman of the board of the firm, filling the vacancy left by J. Leonard Raulston's retirement and resignation from that position.

Mr. Rogers was also re-elected president of the firm and A. A. Kelly will continue as vice president and counsel.

Michael J. Herschel was ap-

(See Page 8, Column 7)

*Stephen Leonard Rogers, Jr. named Chairman of the Board for U.S. Stove Company.*

By 1962, S.L.R., Sr. had retired, and Leonard became president of the company. Longtime friend and attorney Harvey Cameron says Lenny wanted the company to do well for the good of all. "Lenny's compassion for individuals, his desire to make U.S. Stove a profitable company that would be positive for the community, not just South Pittsburg, but for the entire community."

Son Steve remembers that Leonard had a talent for seeing opportunities outside of the traditional stove business. "In 1968, he got interested in buying and selling steel. He built a plant down on the Tennessee River in Bridgeport, Alabama. He connected with a company called Youngstown Steel in Ohio. He was buying scrap steel at cheap prices. It might've been worthless to other companies, but U.S. Stove used so many different gauges of steel that we would sort it and supply our company's production. On top of that, he was able to sell some of this scrap to other companies in the area."

Son Richard says, "He could tell you the current price of any kind of steel right off the top of his head. He'd challenge me with questions like, 'How much does a square foot of 20-gauge steel weigh?' He'd always be challenging and teaching with those kinds of questions. And I learned because of that demanding on-the-job training."

Leonard Rogers had many accomplishments while running the company. Rodger Castleberry says Lenny devised several pieces of the most unique and necessary machinery, including the recoiler and hammer mill. He was an excellent salesman. And he twice saved the company from acquisition.

Steve and Richard remember a time in 1978 when the company was almost sold to the Clark Corporation.

Richard says, "I think he felt trapped and wanted out. I believe our uncle, Bob Thomas, helped our father see that this wouldn't be a good deal for him or the company. They basically were just offering our father a seat on the board of the acquiring company."

Steve adds, "Ultimately, he recognized that it was not a good deal, and he wanted to keep the company in the family. He backed out."

*William F. , Carolyn, Julia W., Anne F., Stephen Leonard Rogers, Jr., Richard B. & Stephen Leonard Rogers, III in 1970.*

There are signs throughout Leonard's life that he was often thinking about his family when he was making business decisions. He created a company called "2554 Real Estate." The number came from his address where he lived with Anne at 2554 Crestwood Drive in Chattanooga.

Steve explains that their dad took out a bank loan for 2554 Real Estate and used the money to buy a rag mill. Then, U.S. Stove leased the rag mill back from 2554. The amount of the lease money paid the note plus $300, which worked out to be $60 extra for each of us five children over the period of time that the company owned it.

Richard remembers that $60 a month made a difference when he was in college. "That's what I got for my allowance. I'd get that at the first of the month. Often I'd gamble it, which was great if I won, but I'd starve the rest of the month if I lost."

Steve says, "We eventually sold it to Lodge Manufacturing for $75,000. Each of the kids got $15,000. Combine that with the fact that he paid for his five children to go through private school and college. That's not cheap. There is no doubt he did care a lot about us."

# Changing Times

When the Arab Oil Embargo came along in 1973, the company suddenly had a huge spike in sales, catapulting itself far past the ten-year steady pace of $3 million a year. At first, abundance rained down on the company. As heating bills brought sticker shock to heating bills, consumers looked to alternative sources to warm their homes.

Son Steve was in charge of the sales department at the time and remembers, "We made the Franklin heaters, and everyone in the world suddenly wanted one. They burned wood and gave customers a big sense of self-reliance. They were highly inefficient, but everyone thought that they were really good to use to survive.

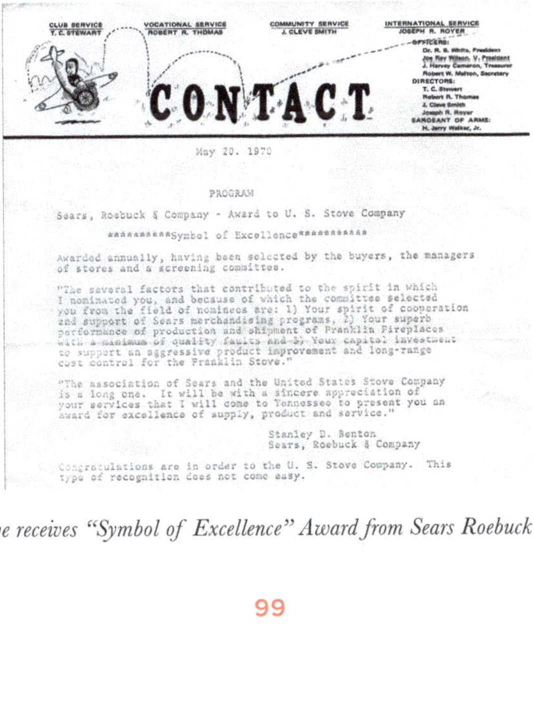

CLUB SERVICE
T. C. STEWART
VOCATIONAL SERVICE
ROBERT R. THOMAS
COMMUNITY SERVICE
J. CLEVE SMITH
INTERNATIONAL SERVICE
JOSEPH R. ROYER

CONTACT

OFFICERS:
Dr. R. B. White, President
Joe Ray Wilson, V. President
J. Harvey Cameron, Treasurer
Robert W. Melton, Secretary
DIRECTORS:
T. C. Stewart
Robert R. Thomas
J. Cleve Smith
Joseph R. Royer
SARGEANT OF ARMS:
H. Jerry Walker, Jr.

May 20. 1970

PROGRAM

Sears, Roebuck & Company - Award to U. S. Stove Company

**********Symbol of Excellence***********

Awarded annually, having been selected by the buyers, the managers of stores and a screening committee.

"The several factors that contributed to the spirit in which I nominated you, and because of which the committee selected you from the field of nominees are: 1) Your spirit of cooperation and support of Sears merchandising programs, 2) Your superb performance of production and shipment of Franklin Fireplaces with a minimum of quality faults and 3) Your capital investment to support an aggressive product improvement and long-range cost control for the Franklin Stove."

"The association of Sears and the United States Stove Company is a long one. It will be with a sincere appreciation of your services that I will come to Tennessee to present you an award for excellence of supply, product and service."

Stanley D. Benton
Sears, Roebuck & Company

Congratulations are in order to the U. S. Stove Company. This type of recognition does not come easy.

*U.S. Stove receives "Symbol of Excellence" Award from Sears Roebuck in 1970.*

Our main customer was still Sears Roebuck, featuring the Franklin heater in the catalogue. They received and sold just about all of our production. They didn't want just truck loads, they wanted trainloads of these heaters.

U.S. Stove simply did not have the production capacity to meet the demand.

Expansion seemed like a natural step. Leonard Rogers decided to buy a large plant in Chattanooga. Steve says, "It seemed like a good idea at the time, but as quickly as the bloom came on the stove market, it came off." The oil embargo ended, the demand for the Franklin stove sunk, and the company was stuck with excess capacity to produce unwanted products.

"On top of that," Steve says, "before 1973, there were twelve companies producing wood stoves in the country, but once the embargo hit, it seemed like everyone who had a garage was manufacturing wood stoves. They didn't care about any EPA requirements. They'd just get in there, weld up a steel box, and sell it."

With demand dropping, U.S. Stove quickly felt the burden of the debt taken on to purchase the factory in Chattanooga.

# The Struggle

There certainly were a lot of great years for Leonard Rogers and his family. He was married to Anne, a woman many loved and respected. He had his five children. U.S. Stove held its own; he was able to start other side businesses with family members like establishing Citizens State Bank with his brother-in-law, Bob Thomas.

Eventually, things began to change.

Son Richard remembered, "Until the time I was about fifteen, I had one of the best childhoods. I don't have any complaints, none at all. But then I saw things start falling apart. I think my father got caught up in the success and status of his position, and in doing so, I think that it changed him. It changed my mom, and it changed the whole dynamics of my family. My little brother got on drugs and had a lot of issues.

My parents always argued late at night. One night, they had a particularly bad argument. And at that time, I was in the ninth grade at the McCallie School. I studied three to four hours every night. It was late, 11:00 or 12:00 at night, when everybody should be asleep, and I heard screaming and a lot of arguing.

I got up and walked into the room and said, 'Do you all realize how stupid this sounds? What's going on?'

My dad looked at me and said, 'Hey you little SOB, if you don't like it, move out.'

I said, 'OK, I will.'

He told me, 'Son I love you, but there's two things I'll do for you. I'll give you a good education, and I'll give you an opportunity.'

I said, 'Dad, that's fair enough.'

So, I moved out. I moved into a place down here in South Pittsburg called 'The Bachelor Quarters.' I was paying $12 a week. There were twelve rooms there, and honestly, the other eleven people who lived in there were pretty much a bunch of drunks. Several of them worked at U.S. Stove. Some of them worked in other places. And so, at an early age, I'm on my own, but not really on my own, my father supported my education, and I was given the opportunity to work at U.S. Stove.

He realized I also had many life lessons to learn. One morning, I was late for work. I had a small room about the size of a jail cell in the Bachelor Quarters. It was near the back door on the second floor. There was a bed, a sink, and that was about it.

I was expected to be at work by 6:00 a.m. It was raining very hard on this particular morning, and I overslept.

Around 6:30 a.m., I heard this loud banging on my door. Then I heard a clicking sound. When I got up on my feet, there was my dad removing the pins on the hinges of my door. He had pulled the door pins from the door and lifted the door right off the hinges!

He told me that if I was ever late to work again, I would

have to move back home to Chattanooga. With that, he grabbed me by the arm, took me to the back door, and slung me out onto the rain-soaked, flat, rubber-coated roof. I slid at least 50 feet in the pouring rain before coming to a halt.

I got on my feet and sloshed through the rain to the back door. I hurriedly got dressed and walked to work. I was about an hour late. I was never late again.

I didn't see it at the time, but as a grown man, I can truly say this was my dad's way of showing me that he loved me. I believe his father showed him the same kind of love.

My father added to my life and work education by basically daring me to do one of the hardest jobs at U.S. Stove. I was earning $1.25 an hour. I remember my first paycheck for a 40-hour work week was $37.22 after taxes.

*U.S. Stove foundry workers catch hot iron from the cupola to make cast iron stove parts.*

That's when I saw these men working in the foundry pouring hot iron. I started asking questions. I learned that these men were being paid by "piecework" rather than by the hour. In other words, they were paid for the number of good cast iron parts that they produced each day.

My dad gave me the chance to try this kind of work while telling me he thought I wouldn't last a week. He knew what he was doing when he told me this. Over the course of my high school and college years, I worked in that foundry and got very good at it. I made $40 per day rather than $40 per week!

I liked the feeling of being my own boss, controlling my destiny. I got paid for the results of my work rather than watching the clock and getting paid by the hour."

## Sons Join the Business

Both Steve and Richard started working at the company as young teenagers. They experienced plenty of hard labor. No favoritism was shown to them for the jobs and tasks they were expected to do, from sweeping floors to any other jobs that needed to be done.

As the oldest son, the one carrying on the name, S.L. Rogers III, "Steve" always understood what was expected of him: working manual jobs, sales, finance, and beyond. Even his college career was spelled out. He says, "I majored in industrial management at the University of Tennessee. The title of that fit right into managing the company. Just look at my name, Stephen Leonard Rogers III. The first ran the company, the second ran the company, why wouldn't they expect the third to do the same?"

*A U.S. Stove employee operates a drill press on a cast iron door for a wood stove.*

There was also the business of the sons fitting in, of gaining respect from their fellow workers, who, of course, knew they were the sons of the boss. Could they stand up to the judgement, the hazing, and the doubt? Richard says he answered that question pretty early on.

"I think I knew at an early age that I was going to be involved in U.S. Stove the rest of my life. I was probably seventeen years old and molding in the foundry making all the various parts for Franklin fireplaces. And all these guys that worked in the foundry, these were just really tough guys out of the hills and mountains around here. They didn't take crap off anybody. There was a particular guy who worked in the foundry in those days, and his name was Cecil Grooms. His nickname was 'Bear.' He weighed about 260 pounds. He was a big old hairy guy who looked like a bear, that's why they called him 'Bear.'

Back then in the foundry, we poured iron by hand ladles making cast iron parts the old-fashioned way with lots of hot, hard, manual labor. I learned how to do that, and I got pretty good at it. And so, all these old guys who have been there many years took offense to a young boy showing them up. If they didn't like you, they'd call you 'a hog.' They would say you are a 'H-O-G' and spell it out in a very unfriendly manner. This guy, Bear, would come over to my area every day where I was doing my job where we'd make the molds.

I'm on the floor going back and forth, digging sand up by hand and putting these molds together. The average worker did maybe 120 a day. I got where I was doing 200 and then even more, and Cecil Grooms would give me crap about it every day, and just berate me every day right before we'd pour it off.

In addition to my work at the foundry, I also had a side job as a commercial fisherman, running trotlines and nets. One Saturday morning, I'm driving to go run my trotlines and my nets. That's when I spot Cecil Grooms standing on the side of the road with a bottle of tequila and some salt and lime. He's motioning to me like he's saying, 'Come over here, you little piss ant. You ain't man enough to stand here and drink some of this tequila with me.'

And this was like on a Saturday, maybe around noon. And so, I pulled over, then I had my little fishing boat behind me that I was going to run my lines with. I said, 'Yeah, I'll have a drink of that with you.'

So, I took a swig, and he looked at me, and he said, 'You know what? I think I'm just going to whip your GD ass.'

I said, 'You know what? I just don't think you can whip my ass.'

Back in those days at the foundry, we wore these boots called, 'gators.' They had steel toes and a leather loop in the back, so that if you poured your shoe full of iron, you could pull it off really easily, which I actually did at least once and nearly lost my foot.

So, Cecil said, 'Let's just go out here in this damn field and settle this.'

We went out in that field, and he beat me so bad. It's the worst ass whipping I've ever had in my life. He had those steel-toed boots on and was kicking me in the face. He broke all my ribs and busted me up very badly.

I'm laying on the ground, he's still kicking and beating me, but I had those steel-toed boots, too. I kicked him just above his ankle on his right leg. It snapped loudly, and I had broken his leg. He fell over. I felt like I was David, and he was Goliath.

As he falls down and pulls out a switchblade knife, and he's crawling towards me, he says, cussing me, that he's going to cut my throat.

There were a couple of guys over there in the field who saw this going on, and they came over there and pulled him off of me. In fact, I think my cousin Reece was there that day, and I think it was Reece who pulled Cecil off of me and kept him from killing me. He was going to cut my throat, I'm sure he was.

This was on that Saturday. On Monday, I'm black and blue, and I can't even hardly see out of my eyes. I went into work and put up my whole job. Bear didn't show up for six weeks. During that six-week period, everybody in the foundry kept saying to me, 'He's going to kill you. He is going to kill you.' They said it so much that I believed them. But I thought, 'Where am I going? Am I going to run? If I run now, I'll be running the rest of my life.'

I knew I was going to stay and face this. Don't get me

wrong. I was scared. I'd be lying if I didn't say how scared I was.

During that six-week period, a terrible thing happened to Cecil Grooms. He lived down in Stevenson, Alabama, about 20 miles away. During that time, Cecil, his wife, and four kids got run over by a train. That wreck killed two or three of his young children. I think that train wreck and his kids getting killed made him change his mind about killing me.

About six weeks later, he showed up at the foundry. He was standing way in the back where nobody else was. I knew this day would come, the day he would kill me or whatever.

So, I'm in the back, and I get this tap on my shoulder. I turned around, it's him, and he's on crutches. I just held my hands up like someone who was surrendering, and I said, 'Bear, here I am.' Honestly, I expected him to shoot me, stab me, or whatever. Instead, he stuck his hand out, looked at me, and said, 'Boy, you're a man, and I respect you.'

That one sentence changed everything. After that, Cecil and I actually became really good friends. In fact, I think it was within a few days that we went and sat on the riverbank. I'll never forget it. We ate pickled pig's feet and drank beer together.

After that, everybody in the foundry and U.S. Stove went, 'You know, hell, he's willing to give his life.' I think I got a great deal of respect because of that. I could tell a big change in the way people looked at me: instead of being

Lenny Rogers' son, I was an independent guy who lives on his own and holds his own.

I know that was a turning point for me where I went, 'Y'know, I think I'm going to stay with this company.'"

## Business and Personal Struggles

While Richard and Steve were becoming men and figuring out their own paths, dad Leonard continued a long decline. The pressures of over-expanding during the Arab Oil Embargo and taking on too much debt took a serious toll.

Steve remembers how sales of the Franklin stove declined along with oil prices. "Even as the sales fell off, they kept producing and sticking the unsold stoves in warehouses. They burned through all the cash that they had. When the smoke cleared, and I found out what had happened, the company had about $8 million in liabilities and about $2 million in assets. We were way underwater."

Longtime friend and employee Rodger Castleberry believes that in some ways, Leonard was brought down simply trying to be a good friend. "In 1973, at the height of the oil crisis, Al Spreen, president of Suburban Manufacturing in Dayton, Tennessee, found himself in a tough spot. His company was focused on making everything for recreational vehicles, something people were not using, because gas was too expensive.

*Ken Woodfin (far right) and Leonard Rogers (second from right.)*

Spreen called his old friend, Lenny. Together, they had owned an airplane. He said, 'Lenny, I'm about to close my doors here.'

Leonard came to the rescue of his old friend. He said, 'I'll tell you what I'll do, Al. We have all we can handle with our Franklin stove production. Our Wonderwood Circulators are coming on like gangbusters. You could produce those.'"

Castleberry cringes at the memory. "Without even a handshake, Lenny turned over Wonderwood production to Suburban in Dayton, Tennessee. Fast forward to 1976, one of our sales reps comes into my office and says, 'Rodger, what do you know about Woodmaster?'

'Who's Woodmaster?' I asked.

'It's made by Suburban up in Dayton.' He showed me catalogs he'd gotten his hands on.

I said, 'My God, it's our Wonderwood!'

When word got back to Lenny, he said, 'I've been screwed.' They had taken our designs and started manufacturing under their own label without any word or compensation to U.S. Stove. We finally got production back the following year, but that betrayal was a devastating hurt to Lenny."

During a manic stage, he bought a company in Bakewell, Tennessee. It was a monstrous manufacturing plant that made pressure vessels and all sorts of equipment for the paving industry. It was so big that when we had our 1976 sales meeting, I chartered a Greyhound bus to hold all of our sales reps. We drove into and around the inside of the facility. It was that big. We never turned on the lights other than that day."

South Pittsburg
HUSTLER
MARION COUNTY'S LEADING NEWSPAPER SINCE 1899
A PRIZE-WINNING NEWSPAPER UT-TPA Press Awards 1978

79th Year – No. 50 South Pittsburg, Tennessee 37380 Thursday, December 14, 1978 15c copy – $6 per year

# U.S. Stove Stops Pouring Cast Iron After 100 Years of Stove Making

### THE SWITCH TO STEEL IS ONLY PART OF THEIR BATTLE TO STAY AT THE TOP OF THE MARKET

**ONCE THE MOLTEN IRON STARTS FLOWING, there is no stopping until all the casts are poured. The molding operation at U. S. Stove, however, will stop the end of this month for good since the rising cost of production has forced the company to turn to alternate products such as steel to stay competitive.**

It's 1:30 p.m in the molding room at U S. Stove. The castings for nearly fifty different stove parts have all been made and are lined in rows across the dirt floor The cupola at the front of the room towers above the activity as everyone prepares their ladels for the hot metal that is about to be poured for casting. A mixture of coke, pig iron, scrap iron, silicon, and gravel has been loaded into the large blast furnace, and in a moment, Billy Campbell, head cupola man for the plant, will ignite the conglomeration and begin the melting process.

At one time, nearly all components for U S. Stove products were made from cast iron. Now, due to changing markets and new designs, more and more of the parts are being made of steel.

With everyone lined up Campbell knocks the earthen plug from the spout of the cupola and the white hot metal begans spilling down into the awaiting containers. The first couple of ladelfuls are poured off since they contain too much slag to be suitable as a good piece of cast iron.

Good, top quality cast iron is what the molders are interested in. They are paid according to the number of approved pieces they produce Molder foreman Bill Gothard says that the number of defective pieces made in the operation is a relatively small percent of total production.

The bubbling metal showers sparks in every direction Protective clothing such as heavy gloves and boots are worn to prevent severe burns. Ironically, strained backs account for more injuries in the operation than burns do according to Campbell.

The molds are made of pressed sand Each molder presses his own molds and fills them with the metal. After cooling, the molds are broken by a shake out crew, consisting of about a dozen high school boys, and the pieces are stacked ready for the grinders to smooth into finished products the next day Tom Hargis is the grinder foreman and oversees about twenty men in his operation. James Ward is the shake out foreman.

The energy crunch in recent years has made wood and coal stoves a very attractive business. On account of that, more than two hundred manufacturers of these products came onto the market in the last two years, plus many other importers, making it a highly competitive and rapidly changing industry Now, to compete in the

*Difficult financial times force shutting of the foundry in December 1978. The next month, S.L.R., Jr. took his own life.*

DUCK KING has been pushing a bull, the large bucket which carries molten metal, at U.S. Stove for nearly thirty years as well as being a molder. The bull rides on a track that extends the length of the molding room so that the molders don't have to travel back and forth so often for more iron from the cupola.

EACH MOLDER at U.S. Stove casts his own molds and pours them himself. They are paid for each piece they produce and the job is considered to be a craft.

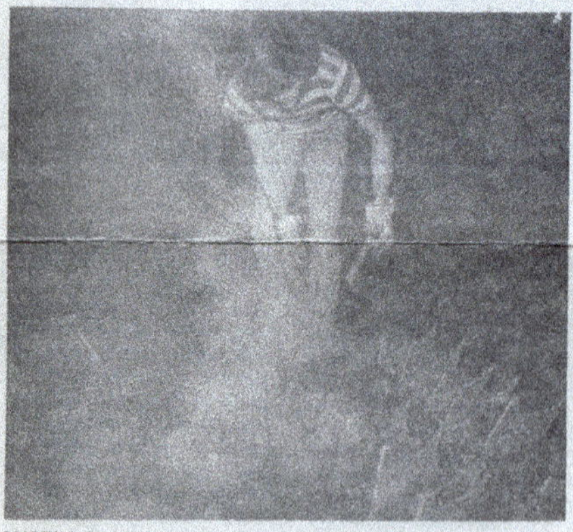

MANY MEN REMEMBER their first job as shake out man at U.S. Stove. The molds are broken and the newly cast pieces set out to be loaded and taken to the grinders. These pieces when smoothed down will be plates for one of the ranges made by the company

marketplace, a company must offer more energy efficient stoves at lower prices.

For instance, the widely popular Franklin Fireplace, manufactured by U S. Stove and distributed by Sears, has gone from a top seller to an item of almost no demand. According to company president Mike Herschel, seventy-five thousand Franklins were produced year before last; this year only seventy-five hundred will be made.

U S. Stove currently employs about six hundred people in plants in South Pittsburg, Bridgeport, Chattanooga, and Bakewell. Herschel says the South Pittsburg plant has, is, and will continue to be the most important plant in the company due to its ability to handle such a wide variety of products.

Although not in desperate straits financially, the company is having to cut production due to an excessive inventory in its warehouses. On account of that, some layoffs have been necessary in each of the four plants and others are coming. Only a temporary measure, Herschel says production at U S. Stove will probably pick back up just as soon as some of the quick newcomers to the market begin to thin out. Two of their young competitors in Chattanooga went under just last week.

Says Herschel, U S. Stove feels that they are an important part of South Pittsburg and they plan to remain so. The foundry will be furbished to handle assembly and storage of other units such as the new Forester Stove, and work will go on at a slightly reduced level until the market stabilizes.

And he added that if they had not been modified to include heat-reflective glass doors, none of them would be sold.

Another factor which has forced itself on the decision makers at U S. Stove is the lower cost of imported cast iron. Already their competitors have turned to this to help them reduce the cost of production. Herschel says U S. Stove has resisted this move in the past, although it has been costly To avoid importing store parts, the company has redesigned as many components as possible to be made of steel in their own plants. Some cast iron pieces will still be used for a while, though, according to Herschel.

The plant will terminate its molding operation at the end of this month. The employees affected will receive benefits from the federal government of up to 80 percent of their income for the following twelve months according to the rules of the Federal Trade Act of 1974 since their jobs were eliminated due to foreign import competition.

Some of the men in the molding department have already left to find other work. Others, like Campbell, who has been with the plant for over thirty years, will work the duration. "When I first came here," said Campbell, "I swore I would never get around the hot metal. Now, I'm the first man to handle it. But I have enjoyed it. You've got to have the 'want to' to do a job right."

Herschel says that phasing out the foundry will involve some of the oldest employees in the foundry, but that it is impossible to ignore the economics any longer He added that the company plans to offer openings in other phases of the operation to these men first as they come available.

U S. Stove is one of the oldest companies in South Pittsburg. The original foundry was built in 1869.

**UNITED STATES STOVE COMPANY**
South Pittsburg, TN 37380
*Home heating made in America since 1869.*

*Photos show how hot and dangerous it was for workers to pour molten iron into molds.*

As the business failures grew, Lenny certainly made huge efforts to save the company. Attorney Harvey Cameron says his longtime friend came to him asking him to buy up stock from various small stockholders. "He wanted to be able to have complete control of the company and not be relying on other shareholders."

No matter how bold and big his efforts were, Lenny's foundation was crumbling as his mental health deteriorated.

Son Steve says, "He was manic depressive. Back at that time, there really wasn't any treatment for that. People said you were crazy. When it got to the manic part, he would self-medicate with alcohol as a lot of people did at the time."

Castleberry agrees, "You can survive one, but the combination of the two illnesses is fatal."

Indeed, Leonard Rogers' personal life had long been in a tailspin. Steve remembers, "He went through a divorce with my mom, and then he got remarried. And when everyone gets remarried, they usually look back and think, 'Oh that was a mistake.' I knew I did. We aren't cut out for marriage. No one in my family is. We have fourteen cousins, and I don't think any one of them is still married to their original person. Anyway, my father got remarried on a rebound, because he still loved my mother."

Upon remarrying, Leonard took $200,000 out of the company to buy a new house for his new wife and himself.

Castleberry says these kinds of moves were catching the attention of bankers. "U.S. Stove was also in trouble with our bank, First Tennessee, in Memphis. They called then-President Mike Herschel and our accountant and said, 'You're going to have to put a tight restraint on Lenny. He cannot continue spending like this.' They called Lenny and told him he could no longer have an active part in the company on order of the bank.

In late 1978, Lenny went into treatment again at a psychiatric hospital in Chattanooga. He stayed for six weeks. When he was released, he came back to immense pressure and fear. Lenny was facing a business that was failing. He understood he had made a lot of bad choices, both personal and professional. It was all too much.

Steve will never forget picking his father up and driving him home. "He told me, 'Steve, the company is broke. There's not but one way out.' I knew he was talking about suicide. He told me that.

It made me very, very mad. I drove him around and talked to him. I said, 'Look, if the company goes under, you can live with me. I can be a plumber or an electrician. We'll make it.'

But he was a proud man. That wasn't going to happen. His second wife said about him, 'Steve, your dad could never have worked for a $30,000 a year job.' It wasn't his lifestyle or the way he was cut out.

I drove him around and calmed down. I went and told the hospital what he had said to me. I called them and said, 'He needs to be back over there.'

They said that they have done everything that they can for him right now. Then it was three or four days later that he committed suicide."

Richard also remembers that day.

"The last time I saw him alive was January 23, 1979. I was on the third floor of our old foundry building. I was actually putting up chicken wire and sweeping the floor and cleaning up to get inventory consolidated into a warehouse. It was going to be collateral for the bank. And I remember that he came up the elevator. It was the same elevator that he rode me on when I was six years old. We'd stop by between Sunday school and church. He would bring me and my brothers down, and we'd ride that elevator.

Anyway, he comes up to the third floor, gets off the elevator, walks by me, and he says, 'Richard, we're not going to make it.'

And I said, 'What do you mean we're not going to make it?'

He said, 'We're not going to make it.' And he just kept walking.

I knew something wasn't right then. As he's walking away from me, I said, 'Hell yes, we're going to make it! Yes, we're going to make it!'

That was the last time I saw him alive.

Rodger Castleberry was the one who told me. He called me and said I needed to go to my father's house in Chattanooga, that something awful had happened. When

I pulled up in front of his house, I saw they were spraying down the driveway where he had taken his life."

## The Brothers' Pledge

The next move the sons made would define their lives and the future of the U.S. Stove Company.

Richard:
*"I left my father's house in Chattanooga and drove back to South Pittsburg. I got a six pack of Miller Lite and went to the river and sat by the river and watched the river roll by. It was raining pretty hard that night. I'm sitting there thinking, 'What am I going to do?' I didn't have any answer. Just, 'What am I going to do?' I was just in total shock. That's when Steve pulled up behind me. I saw the headlights and knew it was him without even seeing whose car it was. We had no cell phones in those days, so he had no way to contact me and tell me he was coming, but I knew it was him."*

Steve:
*"I can't explain exactly how I knew that's where Richard would be. I just knew he would be there and that I had to go to him."*

Richard:

*"I get out of my car in the pouring rain. Steve walked towards me, and I walked towards him. We meet in the middle in a pretty deep mud puddle. We just cried on each other's shoulders in the pouring down rain. I couldn't tell if he was crying more than me, because we both had so much rain all over us.*

*We were both going, 'What are we going to do? What are we going to do? What are we going to do?'*

*That's when I grabbed him by the shoulders, pushed him away, and held him at arm's length. I said, 'By God, I know what I'm going to do. I'm going to work my ass off the rest of my life to restore my family name, and it has nothing to do with money. It has everything to do with pride."*

Steve:

*"We said we were going to bring this company back. It was never about money. It was about family reputation and pride. And we wanted to clear our dad's name, because he owed about everyone in the country. We wanted to pay them off. We didn't want that to be a stain on him.*

*I agreed with Richard. I said, 'I don't give a damn if I ever make a penny doing it. That's what I'm going to do.'"*

Richard:

*"It was about pride in my family, pride in U.S. Stove Company, pride in all the people who worked at U.S. Stove*

*Company, who depend on U.S. Stove Company. Those were the reasons. And it was never chasing the dollar. It was about passion. That's what it was.*

*Over the years after that, there were a lot of things that happened. There were circumstances where I had to go back to that same night and ask myself, 'Why am I doing this?' And the same answer always came true. It was never about the money. It was about trying to restore our family name and going back to doing what was right."*

# 5

# THE GRANDSONS STEP IN

*Stephen Leonard Rogers, III & Richard Barrett Rogers*

It was all well and good for two passionate brothers to make big promises in the middle of a driving rainstorm, but the mess they inherited at U.S. Stove Company was a bigger and deeper mess than the huge dirty mud puddle they stood in the night their father died.

Richard:
*"That's true. It was a big mess. I looked back to when I was a young man, and my dad said he was going to give me an opportunity. I didn't know the opportunity was going to be like that. But guess what? This was an opportunity and challenge. I'm not complaining about it. Luckily, I did get a good education. And if I had not, I don't think that I could have measured up to the challenge."*

Steve:
*"I was 30 years old, and Richard was 25."*

They both had been working in the business since they were teenagers, doing everything from sweeping floors on up.

Was it the plan for either of them to take over the business?

Certainly, neither had ever planned for something like this.

There were plenty of people both inside and outside the company who thought they should not be taking over now, not like this.

The brothers refused to consider any other plan.

## One Step at a Time

The brothers took it one day at a time, one phone call at a time.

First, there was the matter of Leonard Rogers' will.

Steve:

*"The will called for me to be the executor. Pioneer Bank was supposed to be the co-executor, but we owed them $1.8 million. The bank called me up and said, 'We have a conflict of interest here. We can't be co-executor of your dad's will, because there is a lot of debt owed to us.'*

*So, I went to Richard, who agreed to be co-executor with me. He was just a kid. We both were, really. But we worked together. Richard wrote the checks and wrote off the debts of our dad's estate. I tried to figure out how we were going to pay everybody off."*

Richard:

*"I was way too young and didn't have enough experience to understand how bad it was. I'm not sure Steve did either. There was a lot of advice, including plenty of advisors who said we should declare bankruptcy and just basically not pay our creditors and maybe try to go through a restructuring. We refused to do so."*

Richard:

*"Morris Haynie was like an adopted son to my dad. We were*

*in a big meeting with Charlie Fox and Mike Herschel and two or three other executives. Charlie Fox asked, 'Why don't we just declare bankruptcy?' Morris just about jumped across the table and knocked the crap out of Charlie Fox. He needed that, and to be shown the door. There were plenty of guys just riding on payroll.*

*Another one of my jobs after that was dealing with all the people we owed money. I went to the vendors before they came to us. I told them my story, our story, the U.S. Stove story, and said 'You know, we owe you X number of dollars, and we don't have the money. So, you can force us into liquidation or bankruptcy, and you might get a dime on the dollar. But I'm here in front of you to just tell you the intention is to turn this thing around, and all I'm asking for you to do is just give us a chance and believe in us.'*

*Leslie Kellerman at Lodge Manufacturing was one of the primary people who worked with us. I remember Leslie hugging me and crying on my shoulder in the middle of the road on Laurel Avenue up here and saying, 'Richard if there's anything I could ever do, let me know.'*

*Of course, people say that at funerals. I get that. And so, I called in that card, and I said, 'Leslie, do remember what you told me? I'm asking you to give us a chance.' And he did. There were a lot of other vendors we did that with, and their willingness to be patient with us really helped out."*

Steve:

*"We had auditors from all kinds of banks come in there and look. The auditors came in there and shuffled paperwork everywhere, because you didn't have any electronic stuff yet like we do now, and they would lose papers. The next set of auditors would come in and say, 'Where is this documentation?'*

*I would say, 'That asshole who just left has probably got it.'*

*The pressure really hit when our bank called and told us we were being kicked out. Big Ed Simpson at First Tennessee Bank in Memphis was the one who told us we had 90 days to find somebody to help pay off our debt, or they would've taken control, liquidated the company, or whatever they were going to do."*

Richard:

*"It was staggering and overwhelming just to keep the boat floating, just to pay the interest on all the money the company owed. We owed Pioneer Bank $1.8 million on a 30-day note. Those were the kinds of terms my dad agreed to back then. That note went on for years.*

*We went to meet with Bill Hunt from Pioneer. Bill talked to us like redheaded stepchildren. I remember thinking, 'One day I'm going to pay that son of a bitch off and tell him to kiss my ass.' I didn't have the chance. He went to jail for white collar crimes before I could."*

Steve:

*"By the time all the auditors had looked at our finances, only one of them made us a proposal. That was Citicorp. We loaded up in my car and headed down to Atlanta to sign an agreement. We were going to take the only offer we had, a loan for three points over prime.*

*We went in my old Vega, because it got good mileage, and we didn't have much money for gas."*

Richard:

*"At that time, prime was 18%; that meant Citicorp was assuming our debt with a loan at 21%. It was overwhelming just to keep up with paying that interest.*

*Still, we were just so relieved to get the loan. Steve and I were high-fiving each other.*

*We stopped in a convenience store on the way back from Atlanta. I said, 'Steve, let's celebrate. Let's get a six-pack of beer.'*

*I got a six pack out, set it on the counter, and I looked at him, and he looked at me. And I said, 'I don't have any money.'*

*He said, 'I don't either.'*

*So, I took the beer and put it back in the cooler, and we laughed. Here we were. We had got the bank to believe in us enough to loan us millions of dollars, and we thought we had at least enough money to buy a six-pack of beer, but we didn't.*

*From that day forward, we did so many things to just watch pennies, dimes, and nickels. It was just brutal, all the things we had to do that were so unpleasant, but we just had to.*

*Unfortunately, that included layoffs. I think we had 700 employees or thereabouts at that time. We had to shut down a lot of operations and let a lot of people go just to keep the company afloat.*

*We shut down the plant my dad had bought in Bakewell, Tennessee, along with a steel processing operation in Bridgeport, Alabama. We had to consolidate everything from our product line to the number of employees. Everything had to be paired down."*

Steve:
*"Besides the emergency bank loan from Citicorp, ultimately, there were two things that contributed to our success. One of them was actually what our dad said. He had said that suicide was going to help us. I hate it, but he was right. He had a whole life insurance policy that paid about $500,000. And our accountant filed tax forms for tax loss carried back for profits we had paid in previous years, and we got about $1.2 million more. That gave us some breathing room right there."*

Longtime friend and employee Rodger Castleberry has a slightly different version of the sons stepping in. He says Richard and Steve did say they were going to save the company and restore their father's name in a big declaration.

Rodger:
*"They said, 'We are in deep caca. We need to cut expenses. We need to cut this. We need to cut that. And we need more sales.'*

Steve:
*"It took about six years for us to get everything under control. We took it one day at a time; one phone call at a time to the vendors, people that we owed. We stayed in constant contact with them. If you told them that you were going to send them money and you couldn't, you called them back. You'd pester. You keep your word. We kept our word."*

## An Early Sign They Just Might Make It

Steve:
*"The winter of 1979 was extremely cold. Sears Roebuck was our biggest customer, about our only customer, really. They started taking stoves out willy nilly; I mean, it was fantastic.*

*That was another bank we owed money to, but they had a contract. If the contract on a stove was $100, you manufactured it and put it in a warehouse, they gave you $90;*

*90% of that inventory.*

*They are paying on the contract, and that provides cash flow; that, along with my dad's insurance proceeds and the tax law proceeds that our accountant had procured all made for a pretty good war chest. Still, we had all that debt. It was just enough to survive, really."*

Richard:
*"One other thing about Sears. They used to send a lot of returns. For some reason, that year, they didn't send any. It was the same thing the next year."*

Steve:
*"No, they never did. We think that maybe they felt our pain. We'll never know for sure."*

Richard:
*"They did! They were good people. Of course, they are no longer in business. I can say that wasn't a great business decision, but it sure helped us out. It was huge luck for us."*

Steve:
*"That went on for about three years. The winters were cold. That helped with sales, but we didn't have the money to stock up on inventory like you're supposed to do in the stove business."*

Richard:
*"We built gas heaters, and the control valves on those gas heaters were the most expensive part. We'd built all of them, but we didn't have the money to buy the control*

*valves. They'd still be in the box as an unfinished product. We'd buy the control valves when we had the sale because of cash flow."*

Rodger Castleberry believes a major American catastrophe was also key in helping the company turn things around.

Rodger:
*"Three Mile Island turned it around for us. All of the sudden, there was a screaming demand for wood and coal stoves. When that nuclear energy partial meltdown happened in 1979, we were only making 300 Wonderwood stoves a day. But the new demand meant we started making more than 600 Wonderwoods a day, every day of the year, until early 1982."*

*Brothers Steve and Richard Rogers. 1982.*

Steve:
*"It took about three years, but we got those loans paid off. I remember going down to the Pioneer Bank, where I would deal with a woman named Louise Kell. I went down there and made that last payment on that $1.8 million 30-day note. We had the vendors all paid up, banks paid off. Life was good."*

Richard:
*"We got lucky. Well, we worked hard, so I guess we worked hard, got lucky, and got some breaks. I was asked the other day, 'Is our success because of intellect, luck, or what is it?' I attribute a lot of it to luck."*

Steve:
*"Yeah, I do too. It damn sure wasn't intellect. At least not in my case."*

Richard:
*"It would be egotistical to say, 'Yeah it's because I'm so smart.' I just don't think that is the case."*

Steve:
*"Me either. We got lucky. I learned three things during that period you need to manage in order to be successful in business: inventory, interest, and insurance.*

*Because if you get hooked up with an insurance agent,*

*and you become his friend like my dad did with Harold Wilson at Fireman's Fund, they just say, 'Buy insurance.' It gets out of hand. You have to take quotes on your insurance every year.*

*Hopefully, you can avoid debt, which means you don't have interest. And #3 is inventory. It's most important, because the most important thing you can have is cash."*

The brothers believe their father would be proud of them and how they dug the company out of the mess it was in.

Steve:
*"If he came back and was in his right mind, I think he would be proud of us."*

Richard:
*"I agree. If he was in his right mind, he would be proud of our motivations. We wanted to clear his name to the best of our abilities."*

Steve:
*"My dad told me one time that my grandad had asked him a question, 'What's the most valuable thing I have given you?'*

*And my dad said, 'I guess the ability to manage this company. I don't know.' And my grandad said, 'It is a good reputation.'*

*And that is true. That is the best thing you can give a person, to leave them with a good reputation. And then they make their own reputation when they go through life. It's a good start."*

## Turning the Tables

By 1986, U.S. Stove could actually start doing something that would've seemed impossible when they were struggling just to make loan interest payments.

Richard:

*"I actually started looking for acquisitions that would help grow our company.*

*And the first one that we bought was in 1986, a little company out of Mabank, Texas. They made smoker grills. I spent three weeks in Mabank in July, and it was hotter than Hades. But the deal we made was at their place in Mabank, and Mike Herschel then was the president, and Steve, I think, was the VP of Finance. And I don't know, maybe I was some title, I don't remember what it was then. But the guy who owned it, he got up on the table, kicking ashtrays off the table and cussing and raising hell, and just being a complete butthole.*

*Steve and Mike, they were just taken aback. They didn't know what to do. And so I said, 'Hey, we need to have a side meeting. We're going to go out of the room so that Steve, Mike, and I can talk.'*

*We went out of the room. I told Steve and Mike, I said,*

*'Y'all let me take control of this, is that OK?'*

*They said, 'OK.'*

*So, we go back in there, I get up on the damn table, start kicking ashtrays off and cursing him, and telling him to go straight to hell. And I told him, 'Now you know how we got here. I know how to leave and get back where we came from. So, screw you, and we're leaving, bye.'*

*We're going through the airport in Dallas, and the guy comes literally running after us.*

*My little tirade saved a significant amount of money. I'm not going to name the amount, but it was quite a substantial change in what the actual deal was that we thought it was going to be and what it turned out to be.*

*And so we closed that deal, and I moved the business to Chattanooga. Once we were set up, we probably had 20% of the market. The rest of that story comes later in 1990."*

The incredibly hard work Steve and Richard put in to save the company had an added benefit. Steve says, *"It was invaluable helping to keep my mind off my dad's situation."*

Richard agrees. It was as if they could hear their dad's voice in the back of their heads. *"Stay busy. Get to work."*

Steve adds, *"That's what Dad would have wanted. I went into his office after I'd been at the company for a couple of years and told him I needed a raise. His response to me was, 'I'll give you a raise. Off your ass and on your feet.'"*

# 6

# BROTHERS MOVE ON

By 1991, the brothers had accomplished what so many had said would be impossible. They had restored the Rogers family name. They brought the company out of debt. What else could be possible? The answer depended on which brother you asked. For Richard, it seemed the sky was the limit. Steve didn't have the same fire.

He knew for some time that his work with U.S. Stove was done.

Steve:

*"Richard and I have different opinions. Richard is about buying out companies, growing the business. That didn't interest me. I was interested in having a small company and not growth. We were making money, and I was happy.*

*I remember I listened to a tape by Dr. Wayne Dyer, and he said in his tape that the question you need to ask yourself is, 'When do you have enough money? How much is enough money? The amount can't be one dollar more than what you got.'*

*I looked at U.S. Stove, and I looked at my other investments and such, and I said, 'Well, hell, I got enough money. I think I'll just leave.'*

*I told Richard I needed to do something else. I liked accounting. I was good at it, even though that was the one 'F' I got in college. I wanted to do something about that. I went back to study for the CPA exam. I was doing everything they teach you in theory in the academic world, but I had been doing all that in the real world for eleven years."*

Richard:
*"After a lot of conversation and so forth, I just said, 'Steve, here's what I'll do: Why don't you go home for one year and let me run this company, period? At the end of 1991, I will either agree to do the deal with you and buy you out, or we'll both just sell." I was only 36 years old."*

Steve:
*"And that's what I did. I went to school, and that was my job. I remember I took the Becker CPA Course for seventeen weeks on Saturdays from 7:00 a.m. until 5:00 p.m. I was passionate about that stuff. I passed the CPA exam on my first try.*

*Once I had the degree, I knew that wasn't what I wanted to do. I also knew at the end of the year that leaving U.S.*

*Stove was the right thing for me. I told Richard, 'You need to buy me out.'*

*He said, 'We don't have the money for that.'*

*I said, 'This piece of real estate over here. That could be a big chunk of it.'"*

Steve was talking about the big factory their dad had purchased at the height of the Arab oil embargo, the one that had seemed like such a great idea at the time, but had turned out to be a disaster and a huge burden for U.S. Stove. It was of little to no value to the company, but Steve saw a potential treasure for himself.

Steve:

*"It was a wreck when I got it in 1992. I like to work with my hands, so I became a roofer. I became a plumber. I became an electrician. And I fixed it up. It took me about twenty years. Eventually, I got more tenants, smaller spaces as I subdivided. I learned what I was doing. Now it's a money-making machine.*

*Meanwhile, after I left the company, Richard was very successful. He has done a hell of a job."*

But before Richard could be successful, he himself needed to make his own choice. Did he want to buy Steve out? Could he buy Steve out? Was this a company he wanted to run alone? He had some big decisions to make.

Richard:

*"I went deer hunting out on Reece Thomas's farm. I got there when it was still dark, and I was in that tree stand all day long. When I got in that tree stand that morning before it turned daylight, I had made the decision that I had to decide, yes or no. When my foot hit the ground out of that tree stand, I knew that I needed to be fully committed and focused. I sat in that hackberry all day and thought. I literally beat my head against that tree with blood running down my face and onto my clothes. If a deer had run by me, I wouldn't have seen it.*

*It was a tough decision, a very tough decision. I finally came to the conclusion after dark. I'd been up in that deer stand for twelve, thirteen hours, trying to figure it out. All the advisors, all the accountants, attorneys, everybody said, 'Don't do it. It's not worth it.'*

*I finally came to the conclusion that I wasn't going to listen to them. I'd rather try and fail than not try at all. As soon as my foot hit that ground, I said, 'I know where I'm going. I know what I want to do.' I was very, very focused."*

Wanting to buy Steve out and being able to buy Steve out were two different questions. A lucky break and some clever negotiating held the answers.

Richard:

*"During that year that Steve was studying for the CPA, one of my sales guys went into Walmart in Bentonville, Arkansas,*

*where we had about 20% of the business.*

*We were getting ready to own 80% of it, because I had quoted Walmart a price they couldn't refuse. What Walmart didn't know was there was no way I could produce them. Not at all. I took a big gamble, a huge gamble!*

*Backing up about three or four years prior, there was this guy at every trade show who would walk up to the booth and say, 'Hey, I'll give you a million dollars for that business.'*

*Every time, my answer was the same: 'It's not for sale.' This went on for three to four years.*

*I knew this guy was just a front guy for Brinkmann who dominated the market. I knew they were just trying to get rid of a competitor.*

*All of the sudden, Walmart is preparing purchase orders that we know we won't be able to fill without killing ourselves financially. If we did, we would lose so much money because we went in at such a low price.*

*That same guy comes around and says, 'Let's make a deal.' This time I said, 'OK, let's talk.'*

*So, we made a deal. That was one of the primary reasons that at the end of the year I was able to come back to Steve and buy him out like he wanted."*

Richard says this is a good time to mention a man who was key to the success of U.S. Stove over two generations.

Morris Haynie was a young man from Stevenson, Alabama, who started working in the paint shop in the South

Pittsburg plant in the early 1960s. Richard remembers that Morris was a quick learner and very good with numbers. He says, "Morris was extremely good with numbers. My dad's strengths were with language and writing, whereas he always struggled with math. These two complimented each other with their strengths. My father took a liking to Morris and sent Morris to college at Auburn."

Steve remembers that Morris came back to U.S. Stove and started working full-time once he graduated college. "I remember it was 1965, the same year I started working a summer job at the foundry as a sophomore in high school. I worked for him when I joined the company full time in 1971. Morris worked six days a week, always coming in on Saturdays. No one else demonstrated the same interest in the company that Morris did."

Richard adds, "Morris was fiercely loyal, and my dad trusted him unequivocally. I vividly remember a meeting with my father, Morris, and Steve. Our father told us that we needed to accept Morris as our brother.

I was honest with my feelings. Morris was a gruff redneck in many ways. I told my dad that I didn't like the SOB.

I came to find out that I was very wrong. I saw Morris cry so much at my father's funeral that I finally understood how truly loyal he was. After that, Morris and I started to grow closer, and I had new respect for him.

Fast forward to 1991, as I was making my decision to buy out Steve. I went to Morris and asked, 'Are you in this with me?' His positive response was a very big part of my decision to go ahead with the deal.

Everything was set by the end of 1991. Morris became my right-hand man, and I depended on him tremendously as he took over managing the finances at U.S.S.C.

On February 12, 1992, Morris and I were both working at the Richard City offices. As we both left late that day, I told Morris I'd see him the next morning. It never happened. Morris died that night. I was devastated and wasn't sure how I would carry on without him.

With the help of John Hargis and many others, we were able to get through that tough period. I wish Morris was able to see the progress that would come over the next 30 years.

## Foreshadowing?

Steve and Richard's Aunt Ruth believes there might have been some early foreshadowing of who would one day run U.S. Stove.

"One of our strongest family traditions during the time the third generation was young was to celebrate Papa's birthday, every December 23, with a big family dinner. I remember one year when Papa gave each grandchild—there were twelve by then—a $1 bill. As the evening went on, complaints were heard from some of the children. An investigation revealed that Richard and perhaps David

Thomas were talking the younger children into giving them their dollars to be used for some bogus scheme they had cooked up. All the dollars were returned to their rightful owners, but I remember seeing a smile and a twinkle in Papa's eyes at his grandson's eye for making a deal."

Whatever happened as kids, whatever happened as Richard and Steve turned the company around following their father's death, he believes this move to buy out Steve was the right one for the company and their relationship.

Richard:

*"It turned out to be good for both of us and good for the company. During the ten to eleven-year period that Steve and I were 50/50 partners, it had been like a boat with two captains. That was a problem. I'm not saying that I was the right captain, or he was the right captain, but that was the situation. And Steve's extremely conservative, certainly much more than I am. I'm more of a risk taker and a gambler. And so, we kind of had different philosophies on how to grow the business.*

*I was making several acquisitions, and I wanted to make more. In 1988, we had the first one million candlepower spotlight in the country.*

*In 1990, I bought Johnson Energy Systems up in Wisconsin. I saw it as one of the best deals ever for U.S. Stove Company, but Steve "Monday Morning Quarterback" didn't agree with it. He thought it was too risky. He didn't know what a tremendous impact that would make on the company for the next 25–30 years. Truthfully, I couldn't know that for sure at the time, but my gut has proven to be true. It's been one of the most valuable deals ever for the company.*

*It was a product where we were able to dominate a niche market. Then I went and bought two other furnace manufacturers in 1994 and 1996. We had the major share of the wood/coal burning furnace market. Within reason, we were able to pretty much dictate our margins and prices.*

*It was a huge boon to our company. Steve didn't know that, and I sort of did. And so, the deal I made with Steve was to pay him in installments over ten years. Turns out, I was able to pay him in two years, eight years earlier than our agreement called for. I look back now, and that early pay-off seems very similar to the way my grandfather paid off his debt to buy the company three years earlier than his agreement called for back in 1940's."*

Perhaps the biggest gift in Richard buying Steve out of the company was allowing the two of them to do what they do best together—simply be brothers. It is a far better role for them than being business partners.

*Brothers: Richard Barrett Rogers & Stephen Leonard Rogers, III*

Steve:
*"I don't think it is a good idea for a family to be in business together. There's too much room for conflict and too much room to spoil an otherwise good relationship. That's more important than having lots of money.*

Richard:
*"We had different philosophies on how the business should be run. During that period when we were partners, we were both punching time cards. Literally, we were punching timecards, counting the hours we were each at work.*

*That was Steve's idea. He said, 'Let's keep up with the hours that we're at the office working. We'll count the hours at the end of the year. If you're plus or minus, well then we're going to make adjustments per hour.'*

*I said to Steve, 'So when I'm at home, when I'm working, that doesn't count?'*

*He said, 'Nope. It doesn't count.'*

*I had a totally different philosophy of how I wanted this company to work. I said to him, 'I want to get this company working for me instead of me working for it.'*

*He just said, 'Oh no, you can't do that.'*

*I said, 'That is my goal. That's what I want to do. My philosophy was to get the company where it would work for me instead of me working for it.'*

*Whereas the brothers didn't agree on business philosophy,*

*they are 100% aligned on the invaluable brotherhood they have in each other."*

Steve:
*"That's right. Money can't buy that."*

Richard:
*"Yes, I love my brother, I do. He's a great man, as great a man as my grandfather. He is such a good man. He has honesty, integrity, and he's just the real deal."*

The brothers have had challenges and tragedies to face outside of their battles at U.S. Stove. Their youngest sister Carolyn died from throat cancer.

*S.L.R., Sr.'s granddaughter, Carolyn Rogers.*

Their youngest brother, Bill, had a long decline into addiction and mental illness. Steve's daughter, Stephanie, remembers besides her grandfather's suicide, her Uncle Bill's struggles were her introduction to the family's challenge with mental illness.

Stephanie:
*"There was a time in high school when I was at the mall with some friends. I saw my Uncle Bill there.*

*I went up to say hello to him. He obviously was not on his medication. He just kind of stood there and looked at me like he didn't know me. It was very scary. I remember being embarrassed, too. Here I was with all of my friends. They were like, 'Who's that guy?'*

*I just said, 'It's not a big deal. Let's just go, let's just go.'*

*The heartbreaking thing about it is my Uncle Bill was just a kind soul. He was a talented poet. That's the tragic part of it, that he had such a hard time of life."*

Steve adds, "I was informally his caretaker for 25 years. He was a sweet, sweet person. I always said that he was too good for this world, because he was. He would give people the shirt off of his back. He did that all through his whole life, he didn't have anything. But he was a good person. I miss him very much."

*The three surviving siblings of Leonard Rogers: Richard, Julia, and Steve Rogers. 2021. Credit: Jessica Pope.*

# 7

# GOING GLOBAL, ACQUIRING OTHER COMPANIES, FACING NEAR DEATH

As Richard continued to grow U.S. Stove, his brother wasn't the only one who thought about leaving. Longtime supervisor John Hargis had his doubts about staying on. "I didn't think we clicked together, or that he and I could work together. Richard thought we could, but I felt like he was trying to push me out. Now, I can see that he was trying to help me out. Truth is, Richard is the one who put me where I am today.

He's outspoken, and I'm outspoken. We just came to understand that. Everything was transparent. We were broke, and we both knew we were broke. We both knew we had to make something happen. It was Richard's leadership that led us out."

## Going Global

As Richard grew the company, there were some epic deals and acquisitions that will live in company lore forever.

Richard:
*"1999 was a really good one. It was the Ashley Division of Martin Industries. That one was unbelievable. We negotiated all night long, and I got up and left the negotiating table many times. I told them, 'Goodbye,' only to have them come run after me. John Hargis was involved in that one, as well, playing the "cat and mouse" game. At the end of the negotiations, the deal was struck, and the deal was made. It was just unbelievable how it turned out.*

*There have been a lot of good ones. Obviously, you can't win them all, and there have been some that we hadn't done too well with. Some of the deals we've made, we haven't done them justice with our marketing and sales efforts. Some of them were way too complicated with too many models and production problems. Looking back, I can see we should have done many things differently."*

# Near Death

The entire Richard Rogers story nearly came to an early end long before he could fulfill all his potential.

November 11, 1995, Richard went on a hunting trip with his good friend, Mike Barry, and Mike's two young sons, Brandon, age ten, and Jason, age fourteen. That night, they headed to sleep in a cabin on the Barry's property.

Richard:
*"This is a very primitive cabin just built out of plywood, no electricity, not anything in there other than the metal steps."*

Brandon:
*"Jason and Richard were on the wall. Richard was on the floor-level bunk, and Jason was on the top of a bunk, and then there was a door. And then my dad was in a floor-level bunk, and then straight across, I was on the floor-level bunk. There was a woodstove right in the middle of the cabin in between me and my dad."*

Jason:
*"Everybody went to bed. At some point, we heard a rumble over in the distance. It was strange, because it wasn't even raining."*

Richard:
*"We're all asleep about 5:30 that morning, and all of a sudden, all hell breaks loose."*

Brandon:
*"The lightning pulls from the ground, and it comes from the sky, and the energies kind of meet. So, the energy from the ground, you could see where the roots of trees had been blown out of the ground, and it kind of came towards the cabin from multiple directions. Then it was blowing the roots out of the ground, and it grabbed hold of those aluminum steps by us and walked up those steps.*

*From there, the lightning went up a 2x4 and into Richard's foot and then spiraled around his body out of his chest and went up the 2x4 that was behind his head.*

*Then, it basically blew out of the roof of the cabin. Four feet above my head, it blew a hole in the roof. That hole was probably two feet around. "*

Richard:
*"I didn't know this then, but I know now. Lightning comes out of the ground and meets between the ground and the thunder cloud. I just happened to be between the charge coming out of the ground and the one from the sky.*

*It came through my feet through my entire body, blew all my hair off, and set me on fire. Actually, I was dead. The bed was on fire, and I'm dead.*

*The sound woke Jason up. He's in the bunk above me with a hunting vest with high-powered rifle shells in it rolled up for a pillow.*

*The force temporarily knocked Brandon out. Their dad, Mike, was on the ground floor. I think it knocked him out, too."*

Brandon:
*"It was almost like you see in the movies when you see a bomb going off. You wake up, and your ears are ringing. You're kind of blinking your eyes, everything's fuzzy."*

Jason:
*"You got the smell of burning plastic and flesh and all kinds of crazy stuff. I remember you can see where the lightning had come into Richard's body and spiraled out of his clothes. It was insane."*

Brandon:
*"I remember waking up. I was sitting there, kind of addled. The wood stove that we had in the middle of the cabin had a glass front in it. I could see the oddest reflection in that piece of glass. It wasn't flames, but I looked over at Richard and could see this glow. He really was on fire."*

Jason:

*"Yeah, he was on fire. I basically rolled down, and I was like, 'Hey, Richard's on fire! Richard's on fire! Wake up, Richard's on fire!'*

*I rolled him out of his bunk and smothered the fire. The lightning had burned and melted his clothes to his body. He didn't seem to be breathing. I started some kind of CPR based on what we knew about it. I was doing some repetitions on his chest, basic moves I sort of remembered from a magnet my mom had on the refrigerator."*

Richard:

*"I still have shoulder problems today because of the way he yanked me out of the bunk so hard to do CPR. So, while Jason is doing CPR on me, I am basically sitting and levitating 15 feet above the scene. I'm looking down, watching him do CPR on me.*

*I remember traveling through this really calm tunnel. It was just very peaceful. I mean, just amazing. It was quite an out-of-body experience."*

Brandon:

*"I will say it was a substantially long time trying to wake him up. There was a lot of pressure being exerted on his chest, a lot of air getting pushed into his lungs. It seemed like it was taking a long time to have any effect."*

Jason:

*"It didn't seem to have any effect for a little while. And then all of a sudden, he woke up."*

Richard:

*"I remember Mike is standing over me smacking the hell out of me with an open hand, just knocking the heck out of me. And Jason and Brandon's mom, Suzanne, had arrived at the cabin by that time.*

*I look up, and Suzanne is over me. She's crying, and her tears are falling on my face. And I said, 'Suzanne, what happened?'*

*She said, 'Oh, you've been struck by lightning. Don't look down at your chest.'*

*Of course, what's the first thing I'm going to do when someone tells me not to look down at my chest? I looked down, and it looked like somebody had poured pasta and marinara sauce on my chest. There were third degree burns. My clothes were melted on me.*

*I said, 'Oh, no. That's not good.'"*

Brandon:

*"Reviving Richard was just the beginning of our challenges. Maybe just as big was communication. We had none. This might have been our biggest problem of all.*

*We had two-way radios that we always used in our business. Those weren't working that morning. It just so happened, we figured out how to use Richard's cell phone, because he was the only person we knew who had a cell phone, really. I mean, not a bag phone that was in a car, but a real cell phone, which was in your hand. Those phones didn't work really well in the plateau anyways. But we finally got a call in to my mom, and we had to wait for Sewanee Search and Rescue to come in.*

*At that time, the weather started to deteriorate."*

Jason:
*"The bad weather meant the rescuers got stuck."*

Brandon:
*"They got lost and stuck and everything else, because we are about two and a half miles out in the woods. Luckily, Sewanee has an excellent volunteer fire department. They do the training through the university for students. Because of that, they have a training program where they have just more equipment than anybody else in the region has for search and rescue. All the other search and rescue units call those scouts as backup.*

*This meant they were able to get to us eventually. By the time they reached us, my mom was there picking splinters out of Richard from where that 2x4 blew up after the energy left Richard's body."*

Jason:
*"Yeah, that same energy basically went from Richard's head up the wall to my head. I was using my coveralls as a pillow, and I had hunting bullets in the pockets. The lightning melted all the brass in the bullets right under my head.*

*I was trying to keep him calm, which wasn't easy, because after a certain amount of time, he was starting to feel the pain. It was apparent that it was growing more intense.*

*One of our vehicles was dead. Richard's was the only one we could get to start. We really needed to get him out of there. We wrapped him up in sleeping bags and took pillows to secure him in the Suburban SUV."*

Jason:
*"We needed those blankets, because he started getting cold and shivering and possibly going into shock. They just laid him down on the back of the Suburban and took him to where they could get a rescue helicopter to land."*

Brandon:
*"They couldn't get to the actual site, because the weather had deteriorated so much by then that they couldn't land Life Force on top of the plateau, so they had to bring him into Martin Springs and land at a field in Martin Springs before airlifting to Chattanooga.*

*Even then, we barely got out. Within the hour of passing through those roads, they were all blocked from trees that had fallen over. If we'd waited any longer, we wouldn't have been able to get out."*

Brandon:

*"I don't know that we had any more time. He was in pretty bad shape."*

Richard:

*"They shut down the highway, and Life Force picked me up right there on the interstate. They flew me to the burn unit at Erlanger Hospital in Chattanooga.*

*I was in intensive care for eleven days and incapacitated for quite some time after that. The doctors told me, basically, that I would never walk again and that I was pretty messed up. They took skin grafts off my legs to put it on my chest.*

*I think the reason I survived the lightning strike is because before it, I was in pretty good shape. I had just done a couple marathons. I was a runner with a strong heart. Without that kind of conditioning. I don't believe I would have survived. I'd be dead. Running saved my life.*

*But the road to recovery was long and complicated. They told me I had leukemia. You name it, they told me I had all sorts of weird diseases. Frankly, the medical community wasn't knowledgeable about my condition or how to treat it.*

*Then it was, I was going to die of this, or I was going to die from that. The last doctor I saw in Chattanooga had me on so much pain medicine that I was in a wheelchair. I was on some strong stuff. I knew it would be a matter of time before I got hooked on it.*

*I'll never forget it. It was one of those treatment centers where everyone is taking something because they are in immense pain, but it's obvious they're all going to die. I'm looking around in this room, and I'm thinking, 'If I stay here, I'm going to be dead.'*

*I went into that next doctor's appointment and told him, 'I've had it with this; I'm done. Screw you! I'm not taking your medicine anymore.' I was shooting him the bird as I was wheeled out of there.*

*This doctor said, 'Well, if you quit, you're going to swallow your tongue. You're going to have convulsions, and you're going to die.'*

*And I said, 'Hell, you know what? I'd rather die on my own terms than a slow death that you're delivering to me.'*

*Not too long after that, the same guy lost his medical license. I'm no doctor, but I knew he was way over-prescribing pain medicine to all these people. And all the people in there were dying. And so I just decided that if I am going to die, I am going to die on my own terms.*

*Luckily, after that, one of my fraternity brothers was on a beach in Florida and talking to this guy who knew of somebody else who had been struck by lightning. He told him there was this Dr. Hammons at a clinic down in Atlanta. I got an appointment with him at the Emory Clinic.*

*Turns out, he had treated several people who had been*

*struck by lightning. It's kind of strange how I found him, but thank goodness I did, because he changed everything. I was in such terrible shape. Imagine putting an iron skillet on a gas stove turned up on 'High.' Put me in that skillet and just keep flipping me over and over and over day in, day out, day in, day out, so much pain, and it was horrible, truly horrible. I had been in so much pain for so long every single day that I would just sit there and cry, it hurt so bad.*

*Dr. Hammons' approach was more about overall healing instead of just pain management.*

*He prescribed natural herbs, acupuncture, and hypnosis. I tried it all, anything I could to deal with the pain and avoid getting on addictive medications.*

*A week to ten days in, I could see I was starting to get better. My appetite came back. And guess what? I didn't swallow my tongue, go into convulsions, and die.*

*Still when I left that day, I went and met all my buddies and said, "Hey, here's the deal. Let's have one last beer together. Let's go play one more hole of golf."*

*We picked a par 4. I was on a walker, but I could prop up on the walker and at least swing. I got a seven on that hole. I went and did a lot of things. I said, 'This is the last time I'm going to do it.' I was prepared to die. I didn't want to, but I was prepared to.*

*Here's the reason for sharing this whole lightning story: I realized I had reached one of my big business goals. I had told Steve I wanted to get the company set up so it could run without me. I was incapacitated for quite a long time, close to two years. The management team that was there did a really good job. Hats off to them. I had reached my goal that Steve said I wouldn't be able to make happen."*

## Payback

There was another "hats off" gesture important for Richard to remember—Brandon and Jason Barry, who saved his life that day up on the mountain. As the boys got older, Richard told the boys he had something special in mind for them.

Richard:
*"I told them I wanted to help them with college. I didn't completely pay for everything. 'I'm going to help you do this, and I'm going to put this much into it, and I expect you to do the same thing when you get to my age and do it for somebody else.'*

*So, it's more of a passing-it-down-the-line situation. It was never, 'Hey, I'm going to give you this. And this is it.'"*

Brandon:
*"Richard has always been exceptionally generous to people, but he always expects people, when they get to the point where they have the ability to do it, to pay it forward to do just that. So, he's always made that clear to everybody. Generosity breeds generosity. It's just how it works."*

Though it was done from a place of gratitude and generosity, contributing to the Barry boys' college education turned out to be a great investment. One of them is a civil engineer, and the other is a mechanical engineer. Today, in 2020, Brandon Barry is the vice president of Engineering at U.S. Stove Company.

Richard is quick to point out that "Brandon is not just a VP of engineering. He's a really good VP of engineering."

## Stepping Into the Future

The 1990s brought an awareness that it was time to start updating the way U.S. Stove operated. Bringing on new ways of doing things brought its own challenges.

> Richard:
> *"We did it the old-fashioned way for a very long time. I'm proud of that. I also realized technology can make a huge difference. I found that everyone didn't share that belief. It can be very difficult to get everybody to buy into new ways of doing things. That brings down the value of the investment in new technology. I mean you could have a Ferrari, but if somebody doesn't want to drive a Ferrari, they're going to drive a Volkswagen, even if it means producing a lot less. It's what some people are more comfortable with.*
>
> *The new technology that we brought in created new abilities; it helped us run more efficiently to the extent that*

*people were willing to incorporate it. I still don't think we are utilizing all of our technology tools as much as we can.*

*The biggest step in getting ready for the future has been passing the reins to new leadership, to the next generation."*

# 8

# A NEW GENERATION STEPS IN

Richard and Steve come from a family of five siblings, all the direct descendants of S.L. Rogers, Sr. and S.L. Rogers, Jr. Two siblings, Bill and Carolyn, have both passed away. Both had mental health challenges.

Their surviving sister, Julia, had four children. Richard had long seen something special in her oldest boy, who was born September 1, 1979, eight months after his grandfather, Leonard, died. Julia passed on a piece of her father and grandfather by naming her first-born son: August S. L. Jones.

> August S.L. Jones:
> *"My mother was very close to her father and has a deep-rooted connection between him and me. She found out that she was pregnant with me right about the time that he committed suicide. And then nine months later, I was born. So, she has this whole close-knit association with me and him and that sort of thing."*

August's Uncle Richard took notice of his nephew from the time he was a young boy.

*Rock Rogers, August Jones, Mandy Rogers, Sam Paul Jones, Russ Rogers, Stacey and Stephanie Rogers, Christie Jones. 1985*

Richard:
*"I remember seeing him when he was maybe five or six years old, at Steve's house. All the kids were playing on a trampoline. And I've told August many times, and I was just watching all these kids, there was just something about August I just felt. He was observing everything. He was taking it all in, and he*

*wasn't caught up in the moment. He's kind of above the fray, and he sees the whole picture.*

*I was impressed by that from many, many years ago, and I had no idea that someday that he would be involved in the company at all, but he's quite a unique individual. That's been evident from the beginning."*

It's not like August could have just picked up odd jobs as a kid at U.S. Stove. He grew up in Nashville, over a hundred miles away from South Pittsburg.

Still, even there, young August found early opportunities to learn about work.

Julia says she has long seen her son's work ethic: "August has worked since he was eight years old. He has worked more than anybody I have known in my family. He has worked and worked and worked. He learned about businesses. He learned about family businesses from his father's company, Acme Farm Supply. He learned how to work hard, and he learned the mistakes you can make."

*Acme Farm Supply. Nashville, TN, where August Jones started working at 10 years old.*

As a young man, August made his way to the eastern part of the state going to college at the University of Tennessee at Chattanooga. One day, he got a phone call from his Uncle Steve inviting him to come to dinner with him and Richard.

August:
*"It kind of rekindled or kindled that relationship, and the whole story rolls along from there."*

*Richard Rogers, Steve Rogers and nephew August Jones at a charity fundraiser in 2011.*

August is quite honest. Even as he developed a close nephew-uncle relationship with Richard and Steve, working at U.S. Stove was never the plan. Law school was the plan. After he graduated, he was working at a Chattanooga law firm until applying for law school. Even with a plan, he wasn't entirely sure what he wanted to do.

August:

*"I was somewhat perplexed, kind of just in this quandary of, 'I'm not sure what I want. I remember I had this girlfriend who looked at me and said, 'What, do you think some opportunity besides what you're doing is going to fall into your lap?'*

*And I said, 'You know, maybe it will.'*

*Literally that morning, driving to the law firm, I had a Samsung flip phone sitting in my lap, and it rings, and it's Richard. And he said, 'Would you like an opportunity?'*

*I said, 'Well, you know, well sure, what is it?' Obviously, before I just engaged in that, I wanted to know what it was.*

*He said, 'Have you ever thought about working at U.S. Stove?'*

*I said, 'We've talked about it, but I always just kind of figured it was banter. I kind of never thought it was really going to happen.'*

*He said, 'I'd like you to interview with my VP of Sales and Marketing, Rodger Castleberry, and my VP of Manufacturing and Operations, John Hargis.'*

*I simply said, 'I'm up for the challenge. Sure, I'll do it.'*

*I didn't even know what I was interviewing for. At that time, the position that was open was, I believe, a quality inspector. Today, I definitely can read an engineering print, but then, that wasn't really my wheelhouse. So, you know, I asked Richard, I said, 'What am I interviewing for?'*

*He said, 'Something like a Quality Control Inspector.'*

*I just said 'OK. I mean I'm not sure what that means, but I'll go for it.'*

*There was also this underlying suggestion of, 'That's what you're interviewing for, but you're actually interviewing to come on to cut your teeth. You may have to sweep floors, but who knows what you're going to be.'*

*I sat down in John Hargis' office in Bridgeport, Alabama, with Rodger Castleberry sitting across from me. As the conversation went on, I flat-out asked, 'What am I interviewing for?'*

*John said, 'Well, I think you're interviewing for a Quality Control position, but I'm not sure if that's really what you're interviewing for.' And he said, 'You know, some of the waters are muddy, you know, Richard has two sons who haven't shown enough interest to take over the company. So, here we are.'*

*And I said, 'All I can ask is judge me based on me. Whatever somebody else has done, that's what they've done. Give me an opportunity to be judged upon my own representation of myself, not what somebody else has done, not even Richard.'*

*He said, 'I can appreciate that.' Then he leaned back in*

*his chair and asked, 'Where do you see yourself two years from now?'*

*And I'm going to quote this. I said, 'Sitting in your fucking chair.' I'm not going to lie, at that moment I realized I had literally put everything on the table. Everyone was just sitting there. There was no gray area. Either I just completely fudged this thing, or it was a slam dunk. I had no idea.*

*John rocked back in his chair, rocked back up, and simply said, 'When can you start?'*

*That's how I started working at U.S. Stove on April 4, 2004."*

## A Humble Beginning

August:
*"I showed up for my first day in frayed jeans that were too long, a long-sleeved shirt, and work boots. I swept the entire warehouse for the first week that I was there. That's all I did. Then, I kind of moved on to the steel room, where I sliced my finger open handling raw steel, and got to learn about that. I literally worked my way through the entire manufacturing process. There still isn't any job function as far as from a production standpoint that I haven't performed."*

There were other important lessons for August to learn about the culture of U.S. Stove and the surrounding area. John Hargis played a key role.

*August Jones and John Hargis. 2021. Credit: Jessica Pope.*

August:

*"I continue to get a lot of grief about this. When I first started at U.S. Stove, I had a debit card. I didn't carry cash. Well, the local restaurants in the area didn't take debit cards in Bridgeport, Alabama. My boss, John Hargis, had cash, and for three to four weeks, he'd buy my lunch and breakfast. Finally, he had enough of that. He schooled me. He finally said, 'Son, I'm telling you what. That card isn't going to get you anywhere. You better start showing up with cash, because I'm tired of paying for your lunch.'*

*That was the day I started carrying cash.*

*I evolved through the company—moving up to Director of Manufacturing and Chief Operating Officer. Even today, I could still walk through our manufacturing facility, and I could take somebody's job away and do it for them. That obviously gave me a lot of respect, too, because the people knew that I could work at any position in the manufacturing process.*

*It's been straight-up vertical. There was no gradual process. I walked into something that I knew nothing about. I knew a little bit about business. I had worked in my dad's feed store when I was young. He let me even do payroll when I was eleven years old. So, I understood the concept of business, but I don't have a business background. I didn't know what a P&L was, I didn't know what a sales forecast was, I didn't know production scheduling or bill of materials. I couldn't read an engineering print when I was first handed one. It took me a while to figure it out. I literally had zero experience as far as the business goes."*

Beyond not knowing business, August didn't know this business.

August:
*"I didn't know what a pellet was. I barely knew what a stove was."*

Then there was the challenge of being the president's nephew.

August:
*"When I came on, I didn't want it to be known that I was Richard's nephew. I knew there would be a stigma with that. And I had the added challenge, because people would say, 'Here's this guy who has no experience, coming from a legal background. He's going to go to school, and now he's all of a sudden coming in. Clearly, he's handpicked to be the Chosen One.'*

*That was the sort of thing I was hoping to avoid, so when I first came in, I took advantage of my last name being 'Jones' and not 'Rogers.' I really wanted to make sure that nobody knew that I was Richard's nephew. Well, that lasted twelve hours, or maybe it was five minutes. Once it was known, it became a burden, because everybody did look at it and say,*

*'Well, that's Richard's nephew. This is just handing over a silver spoon and just giving it to somebody who's not going to work for it and doesn't know what they're doing. It's just this lineage situation.'*

*That only drove me even harder, because that was completely opposite of what the reality was. Richard will be the first person to tell you he didn't hand anything to me. He gave me an opportunity, one that was mine for the taking. It was never, 'Hey, you come in, and now you are the president of U.S. Stove Company, where you just put on a suit and show up for work.'*

*No, it was understood that I better show up for work and negotiate my way through every pay scale and every title.*

*In some ways, I think being the nephew was almost worse than being the son of the owner, because it was like, 'He's not even the son, and the owner is going to bequeath all this to him?'*

*So, yeah, I got a lot of grief on the floor when I was working with the other employees. Some would say, 'Hey, Nephew.'*

*There was a lot of that, but as I progressed and worked with all those employees, I gained respect for being me, not being just the nephew. From my first day, I created and started defining who I was, not based off of who Richard, Steve, my grandfather, or great-grandfather was. It was my own legacy I was creating.*

*I worked on the floor with all the employees forming friendships and professional partnerships. We'd have coffee before the bell rang. We'd have lunch together. If I forgot my lunch, somebody would have a bologna sandwich. I got to be respected on a level with our employees that kind of dispelled the stigma of, 'Oh, that's just his nephew.' My coworkers could see I was earning my keep."*

## The Union Goes Out

As I started progressing through the ranks, I started drifting off the floor. I'm spending more time in the office, and I'm doing more production planning, and I'm running all of these types of things. I'm still running things to the floor, but it's understood that this is a transition. The employees respected that from a standpoint that they knew I could still get out there and do it.

We were unionized at that time. The fact that the employees voted the union out meant my relationship with them and our mutual respect for each other was crucial.

Let me be clear: I didn't get rid of the union, the employees got rid of the union; they had options. It came down to two simple questions I was able to put before our employees, 'Do you believe in what I'm bringing, and what I can bring to the table? And is it better than what they're negotiating for you?'

Turns out the answer to the question meant the employees trusted me more than they trusted union leadership. That trust, that act of faith, has to be one of the highest compliments I've ever received in my life.

When I came on in manufacturing, there were probably about 120 full-time employees who were available to join the union, the International Brotherhood of Boilermakers. About 70% of the workers joined. A lot of the younger people did not. The union still had to represent them even if they didn't pay dues, so a lot of the young guys were like, 'Why am I going to spend money when I can get it for free?'

I inherited a union contract when I first came on. We were pretty much in the final stages of sealing the deal. In my opinion, there were lots of bad parts of it. This is actually how I came to become the personnel manager.

## Instant Promotion

I was sweeping in the paint department when John Hargis pulled me off the floor. He had heard that I had a limited legal background. He pulls me in and asks, 'What do you know about contracts?'

I said, 'Well, I mean, I know about contracts.' He said, 'Here's a union contract.'

I said, 'OK...'

He said, 'Here's a grievance. We have a meeting in twenty minutes. I want you to answer it.'

I literally had twenty minutes to read the union contract, apply everything in the contract to the grievance that was filed by an employee, and respond to the grievance in writing. Then I had to meet with the union and their international rep who had flown in from Oxford, Mississippi.

The guy gets bent out of shape, because I said, 'Well, this is what it is, this is what it says. I don't have an opinion. I don't know this person. I'm just telling you this is what it is.'

So sure, he gets bent out of shape. He's there to represent this employee. Of course, he has to believe that she's right. I understood that. I wasn't offering a subjective opinion, just stating the facts and situation as it was and how it related to the union contract.

The union rep protested, 'She's going to lose her job.'

I replied, 'I can't help that. It's what the contract says. She's going to lose her job, because that's what you all agreed to. I had nothing to do with that.'

Then he pulls the title card. 'The contract says here that only the plant manager or personnel manager can answer these grievances. Who is this guy?' He pointed at me.

John Hargis looks at me, looks at him, and says, 'I guess he's the personnel manager.'

No one was more shocked than I was to hear this news. Well, maybe the union rep was. He certainly was suspicious.

'Well, does he have a business card?' he demanded.

'No, but he will,' John Hargis replied without hesitating.

And that's the story of how I got promoted to Personnel Manager, my first official position at U.S. Stove.

As that union contract expired, I inherited all that went with it. At any given point, I was probably getting six to ten grievances a week. I was doing my best to answer all of them.

I took it on as this challenge; banter back and forth between the stewards and myself and their union reps. I took on the harassment of being the young kid, the nephew, the 'He thinks he's a legal whipper-snapper.'

We got through that contract. I negotiated the next one, which was more in line, and we went through it all again as we approached the next one. It was four long years of this.

With each of the contracts, health care was always a big, big issue, and at that time, it was just incredibly crazy. Rates were through the roof. What we had previously agreed to was no longer sustainable. We just couldn't do it anymore. It was a huge sticking point in the negotiations.

Over the course of this, I kept a dialogue with the membership employees. I told them, 'We keep spending more time, more effort, and more energy on trying to negotiate something that's actually not beneficial to you.'

I didn't want to say anything more than 'This is so foolish, nickel-wise-dollar-foolish.' You've got categories of employees being paid less than others. When you try to give them more money here, they didn't want to take it over here, because they weren't senior employees. It was just irrational to me.

I was trying to explain some of this to them. One day during a casual lunch conversation, I said in passing, 'You know, I think I could do better for you all as employees if I didn't have those handcuffs. I know you think they are supposed to help me help you, but they are actually hindering me. I would love to do more for you, but I have to abide by the contract. The contract works both ways. It protects you, but it protects us. And it also creates definitions and parameters and boundaries that neither side can bend. You know there is no gray. It literally is black and white. If that black and white is gone, then there's gray, and then there's also an opportunity to do more.'

That kind of opened a door, and we started to have a lot more of these kinds of conversations even while we were at an impasse in the negotiations.

## Lucky Horseshoes

*Actual horseshoes used in epic game.*

It helps to be on what I believe was the right side of the union debate. I'm also thankful for a little luck that came my way.

The height of our union contract negotiations happened to fall just as our town was gathering for our annual Cornbread Festival. This is a big deal where the whole town comes out to gather and celebrate each April. I was hanging out at these big horseshoe pits by the old foundry. Let me just say that there are people like Richard who have played horseshoes their whole life and are really good at it. Then there are people like me. I've barely played, and I'm not kidding when I say I'm terrible.

I spotted James Spangler hanging around the horseshoe pits, as well. James was a well-respected U.S. Stove employee, a lifetime union man, a true leader with an unforgettable gruff voice. James and I decided to play horseshoes together.

This, no doubt, was not my smartest move. I knew James was really good at horseshoes. Pretty much everyone knew I was terrible. Things started out about like you might expect. He was kicking my tail. For some reason I thought it would be a good idea to add a wager on this match.

I dared him, 'If I throw a couple of ringers, you have to get up on a picnic table and tell everybody what a good place the company is and what a bad thing it is for the people to be unionized. You're really going to have to preach this.'

He and I were standing there, I took one of his Pall Mall

cigarettes, and we got the game going. I picked up one of the horseshoes and tossed it. This is where Richard and I disagree on telling this story. I think I looked pretty graceful throwing that thing. Richard swears it looked like a wounded duck falling out of the sky.

However I threw it, that horseshoe went around the pole! I shifted hands and launched the other shoe. Again, Richard says it was the ugliest throw he'd ever seen with no form or turn.

I don't know what I would call it. But I do know that the craziest thing happened. It was like something grabbed that horseshoe out of the sky and shoved it down on that pole.

By this time, there was a crowd gathered around. James Spangler couldn't believe what he was seeing. I just took a puff of the cigarette, put it out on the ground, and said, 'Well, I guess that settles that.'

Let me just say long before this miracle horseshoe match, Spangler and I had a really good relationship. I drank coffee with him in the morning and stuff like that. He and I liked to talk a whole lot of trash. Bottom line, he was a good man, a man of his word.

Sure enough, he went to the Marion County Park where the union members used to have their meetings. He got up on a picnic table and pretty much told the entire union membership that they needed to get rid of the union.

Honestly, he didn't make this grand gesture just because he lost the bet. He did it because he definitely believed that the non-union way was going to be the better path for the people. He and I had a sidebar conversation where he looked at me and said so. He looked me straight in the eye and insisted, 'You better stick to your word and make sure that these people are taken care of with their wages and that they're treated the right way. This better not work out poorly.'

I wasn't there that day in the park, but I'm told James Spangler got up on that picnic table and told his fellow union members, 'We need to get rid of this. We need to trust August.'

Within the week of Spangler making that speech, the momentum shifted, and the membership completely changed direction. The union rep became less and less available. I knew something was going on. Finally, the union rep had to reluctantly admit that the union had filed a disclaimer of interest.

*International Brotherhood of*

**BOILERMAKERS • IRON SHIP BUILDERS BLACKSMITHS • FORGERS & HELPERS**

*753 State Avenue* *Kansas City, Kansas 66101-2511*

NEWTON B. JONES
INTERNATIONAL PRESIDENT
WILLIAM T. CREEDEN
INTERNATIONAL SECRETARY-TREASURER
913/371-2640

J. T. RHEA
INTERNATIONAL REPRESENTATIVE
GENERAL ORGANIZER
P.O. BOX 241
WEST POINT, MS 39773
OFFICE PHONE: 662-494-9132
OFFICE FAX: 662-495-0090
MOBILE: 662-889-9975
E-MAIL: jtrhea@boilermakers.org

February 2, 2011

Mr. Ronald K. Hooks, RD
National Labor Relations Board
80 Monroe Avenue
Memphis, TN 38103-2481

RE: DISCLAIMER OF INTEREST

Mr. Hooks,

Please find enclosed a signed and dated DISCLAIMER OF INTEREST regarding Local Lodge S-56.

My contact information is;

James T. Rhea, IR-ISO
Boilermakers
P.O. Box 241
West Point, MS 39773-8110

Phone – 662-494-9132 (O) 662-889-9975 (M)
Fax - 662-495-0090
Email – jtrhea@boilermakers.org

Respectfully submitted,

James T. Rhea

James T. Rhea, IR-ISO
Boilermakers

*The National Labor Relations Board officially ends union representation for U.S. Stove employees. February 2011.*

Moving on without the union is something ownership and management had worked on for decades. Do I get credit? Definitely some. Richard swears the change started to happen with that one horseshoe match.

In any case, I know to quit while I'm ahead. Those specific horseshoes have a place of honor sitting on my console. And I haven't played a match since that day.

It's moments like this that test me as a leader and simply as a human being. Every single one of those people I've worked with, grown up with. Many are personal friends. I have to take those relationships into account in my decision making, but I can't let those relationships affect the direction the company needs to take.

I can't say enough how much their trust in me means to me. I put my word on the line to them that I would do right by them, I would do better for them. I was talking about better wages, better company morale.

For those first five years that we came out of the gate, there was nothing but adulation and pats on my back. I could walk through the plant, and there was no more 'Us against them.' It was just, "Us." All the people that were on the floor, who used to feel like they were ostracized, that they were independent of the company, those people suddenly felt unity.

No one would look at me and think, 'He's not allowed to drive a forklift, because that's not his job.' All of the sudden, everybody's job became everybody's job. Their job was the same as everyone else's. It was about answering the question, 'How do we become successful? How do we contribute to the company? Because if the company's successful, and the company is making money, we're all making money. That's what we are here for.'

Then, there's also like these secondary levels of enjoyment that could come along with the job. It's one to be able to go to a job and get paid. It's something even better to be able to go to a job, get paid, and love going to the job.

That's the kind of mentality that I wanted to create, and I did create. And all the employees embraced it and wrapped their heads around it.

It's part of the next evolution of this company and this family. Steve and Richard have their own war stories of dealing with the union. I shouted to them, 'Listen to the fourth generation. We got it done.'

However it came about, I now know for sure what I long suspected. Moving on past the union wasn't an option, it was crucial. I can honestly say this without any doubt, we wouldn't be in business if we still had a union. The rapidly changing demands of consumerism with respect to the competitive landscape, with respect to product innovation, even manufacturing capabilities, means we absolutely have to have flexibility.

We were handcuffed with these black and white agreements. The fact that they were done in four-year increments was even crazier when you consider how quickly the world is changing right now. 2020 has been that and more.

We've been non-union for four years. It has given us the versatility to evolve and adapt as a company and to make changes where we needed to change them. We went from a company that was isolated to a certain product category with manufacturing restraints to one that could maneuver to a shifting marketplace.

We brought in Trumpf lasers, we brought in high-level technology and cutting and bending capabilities, we overhauled personnel. I was able to be versatile, moving people from one role to another and not have to put in a change request or that sort of thing.

It gave us what we needed to be a company to be able to adapt to some rapidly changing conditions.

They've gotten even crazier in the past five years. We went from this old cookie-cutter process to all of a sudden, we have flexibility. We're creating new products, innovative products, and patents. I drew stuff up on napkins that now have some US patents on them. Obviously, the company owns the patents, but I take great pride that they are in my name. None of the things that we have done now could have been done with those parameters set around them."

Director of Manufacturing, Gerald Hargis agrees. He says he wouldn't have agreed to join the company in 2011, if there still was a union.

Gerald Hargis:

*"I think unions were great in their day, but I really don't think that in today's world, Union representation does not stand for the working man, in my opinion. And I've been on both sides, but in today's world, there's a lot of political stuff involved in unions. They're more out for themselves and how much money they can make for the union."*

## Meeting New Challenges

The current leadership has a whole other layer of challenges: changing old products and designing new products to fit EPA standards.

August:

*"The first three generations didn't even have government safety levels they had to meet. Their mission was just to throw a log on the fire and burn it. Now there's 'grams of particulates per hour' that are measurable.*

*We have a state of that art test lab that was instrumental in creating new products. We brought in third-party organizations into our state-of-the-art test labs. It's laughable that something like this would exist here 20–30 years ago.*

*They were just, 'That's so crazy. Why would you even have that?'*

*When I first started at U.S. Stove, our engineering department consisted of only five people. It was like there was a model shop maker, a designer, and somebody to help with some CAD drawings. That was pretty much it. It was a very limited staff.*

*Now, we have a state-of-the-art team of engineers and designers. We do 3D modeling with plastic. We built a little replica stove sitting there in the lab so that the EPA can see that it's up to standards. That was one of the biggest challenges. Getting the exit of the union and allowing us to be a more versatile and nebulous company was huge. Our ability to reinvent our products in the face of the EPA and what they were bringing to the table. Without that we would 100% be out of business."*

Brandon Barry is the current Vice President of Engineering at U.S. Stove, the same Brandon Barry who helped save Richard's life, only now he's all grown up.

He teamed up with August in realigning the entire company catalog of products needed to be looked at, revamped, brought up to date, or discontinued. He and his team have had to do this in a ridiculous amount of time.

Brandon Barry:
*"In 2014, we had our hands in just about every category of wood-burning products out there. They all fell under a new regulation in 2015. August and I sat down and realized, 'How are we going to get through this? Because we have products that are not certified, they're not clean burning.*

*We're going to have to redesign all of these.'*

*2015 was just a start. We had to get a certain amount of products that were compliant with 2015 regulations. Everything that we offered had to be certified as clean burning by 2020.*

*Just to give you an idea of what that entails. It takes anywhere from twelve to eighteen months to design, test, and certify wood-burning products. We took a lot of those down to the six to eight-month timeframe. From 2015–2020, we basically had to put together a strategic plan and say, 'We're going to certify this group of products, this group of products, this group of products, and go through them all.'*

*We also made a strategic plan to maintain revenue, while getting compliant with regulations, all the way up to where we are today. We got back our last certificate from the EPA the week before selling season began on Labor Day.*

*It's been a journey. I always tell August we put together a strategic plan and stuck to it. And we are a viable company today. There are a lot of companies that are not going to be able to say that in the next year or so.*

*I'm not exaggerating when I say you can compare this to climbing Everest. You gotta do it one step at a time, or like eating an elephant, you just eat it one bite at a time. That's what we had to do. We really had to plan and be logical.*

*We had to keep moving forward while in the background; we, along with our trade association, were suing the EPA. We were fighting these regulations because we felt they were not legally justified by the Clean Air Act. We fought it the way through, thinking, hoping, maybe we'd get some relief. Ultimately, we didn't get that relief, so it's a good thing we never stopped pushing ahead with our revisions and redesigns.*

*It has also meant letting go of some parts of the business that would have never been up for discussion."*

August:

*"Our furnace business, which was at one point like 50% of what drove us as a company, is now zero."*

Brandon:

*"Yes, you can say we've lost a whole category of products, which are wood furnaces, but it's really a two-sided conversation. Yeah, we lost them, but if you look at energy costs today, it's more cost-effective to buy a natural gas product or a more efficient electric product today than it is to buy a wood furnace if you're running a central heating system. We were just listening to the marketplace, which was continuing to dwindle. That's why we decided to not certify a product for that category, at least not this year. I think it's going to pan out to be a good decision. But if you looked at that business several years ago and heard about this decision, you would think we were nuts. It was a big hit to our company, but we had to plan and make that decision. We couldn't bet on keeping that product category with our challenge against EPA regulations.*

*Meanwhile, look at what U.S. Stove has now.*

*When I first started at U.S. Stove, we had one modern EPA certified wood stove. Today, we have the second largest group of EPA certified wood stoves of any other manufacturer in the industry. So, we've come a long way as a company, in terms of our product offering, in terms of being able to comply with regulations and be a leader in the industry.*

*We have three of the top ten cleanest burning non-catalytic wood stoves in the marketplace right now. So, it's pretty neat to see a department that only had one stove to offer at that point when I came onboard that was EPA certified. And you didn't have to have everything EPA certified. So, we made a lot of other products. But the regulations have tightened down so much in the past twelve years since I've worked here that we are to the point where everything has to be certified. And we have the second largest product offering for that.*

*Today we're focused on building cost-effective appliances whether they are furnaces or stoves. The guys on the assembly line used to say, 'We're not building rocket ships.'*

*Today, all the steel we use is laser cut. All the cast iron is precision poured. So, it's not quite as complex, but, yeah, today, we are actually building rocket ships. It's a huge step from where we were twelve years ago to where we are today."*

Richard:
*"The pie might have shrunk, and I think it has shrunk, it's not as big as it used to be, the total market. But our market share*

*has grown, because the competitors have not been willing to invest or made a decision not to invest in the future because of these regulations. This is where Brandon comes in. He has revamped our entire product line. Because of August and Brandon, we have a complete offering of 2020 compliant products that very few others have. I think the future looks really good, I really do. So yes, I think the future's bright."*

While August and Brandon knew all along these were crucial investments and hard choices, they have not always been an easy sale.

August:
*"My wish list was long, and some would say expensive. A better engineering department, better resources, bringing in personnel that were qualified. We brought in a team of people from the outside and brought them in-house. It was a gamble because you're adding overhead, and then there's the expense. And engineering is one of those funny ROIs that when you present it to a board of directors, it's like marketing. There's some smoke and mirrors to it. When you sell a product, what your profit is. You can invest in products. Trying to show where that ROI is a little more difficult.*

*But, you know, Richard has been fully supportive along the way, and so we brought in some great personnel and resources. The products that we offer today, none of those were offered five years ago. We're the most diverse company in our entire industry as far as product offering. But nothing, nothing was available five years ago."*

Richard:
*"I appreciate the steep hill that August, Brandon, and the company has had to climb. I'm all for clean burning and clean water, clean air, I'm all for that. But to put the burden of all these EPA regulations in perspective, back in the early 1960s, 1970s, there were twelve big companies in this business. We called them 'The Dirty Dozen.' Then the industry grew like crazy in the early 1970s—companies trying to take advantage of the Arab oil embargo. There were probably more than 500.*

*What the EPA has done has wiped out 90% of the companies in this business. Now there are really only five to ten companies still in this business. It's just too hard and expensive to meet all the criteria and still make a profit."*

The fact that August has been able to steer the company to this point of surviving and thriving is why Richard turned over the reins and has August now president, running the entire company, something August had been gunning for since that first interview with John Hargis.

## The Pandemic Brings Even More Challenges and Opportunities

Just as the company team was rounding the corner of redesigning all the products and bringing them up to code, along comes the historic coronavirus pandemic, devastating from a health perspective, just as fatal to many American businesses.

August:
*"We were coming off the heels of a transition from non-2020 compliant product into 2020-compliant product. I was managing the supply chain at the retail level but also managing the supply chain from our vendors and factories, literally knowing everything in this basket is no longer going to fit into this basket. It's all expiring. And whatever's left in this is bad. I can't do anything with it."*

But something even bigger soon caught August's eye. Long before most of the country had an inkling of how life was about to change in previously unimaginable ways, early signs were coming into company headquarters in South Pittsburg from a world away.

August:
*"We have an entire supply chain team on the ground in China currently, and they gave us a heads-up. There were a lot of*

*things that we had to do from a supply chain standpoint.*

*In any given year, we would make adjustments early in the year because of Chinese New Year. Going into 2020, we could see this was going to be some bad stuff. I knew I had to adjust plans we already had in place. We had to advance and bring more in instead of being cautious and getting caught short on supplies.*

*We also had the benefit of being a seasonal business. From a supply chain standpoint, this started hitting in January. Our big sales season isn't until after Labor Day. That gave us time to see how this pandemic would affect other businesses and help us adjust ours.*

*As devastating and awful as this pandemic has been, the truth is, it has also been a huge opportunity for some businesses. Early in the spring, we saw some companies catch fire—companies like Peloton, home gyms, Zoom, delivery services, basically, anything that had to do with making life better when you stayed at home. I was determined that was going to be the case for U.S. Stove when our high season came around.*

*I decided we would just pump it up and bring everything in. We went from kind of the 35-mile-per-hour zone to pressing our foot to the gas. Let's see what the governor is on this thing and move the needle. So, we did that, so there was a lot of investment that went into that. At that time, in the early months of the year, that's just abnormal. I didn't have a whole lot of time to sit there and say, "Well, let's do a great deal of analysis." This is, you know that's leadership in this moment. It's, 'I don't have time to sit there and spend two weeks doing, why should I, shouldn't I, should I?' Simply, 'It's you.'*

*Some of it's got to roll, and you have to react and all of that. Your gut is led by what you already know, and it's kind of a feeling.*

*Going into Spring 2020, we weren't affected too much. We were carrying greater inventory, which caused an impact to P&L, but I just had to ride that and explain to Richard that I believed I was making the right moves. I call him the 'Monday Morning Quarterback.' He's asking questions, and I'm having to tell him that I know it doesn't look good, but trust me, it's not bad. And just because it doesn't look good doesn't mean there isn't a plan.*

*January was just literally an 'Oh Shit' moment, where I'm just going, 'If I don't hold the reins on this, if I don't breathe a little bit and make sure that I'm managing all those spinning plates and making sure that each one of them is being set down on the table, they're all going to start breaking.'*

*Everybody knows 2020 has been tumultuous and for obvious reasons. But it's been one hell of a ride."*

## Seeing the Opportunity

August:

*"I also looked at this as an opportunity for the company. How lean can we get and still function? Where are the pain points? And if we're going to expose them, reduce the overhead, and now we're being forced to. So, the pandemic, to me, wasn't a point of pain. It was a point of opportunity to literally let the water erode, let's look at the gravel here and see what's making us tick. This was a tremendous opportunity to do a SWOT analysis of the entire company. Strengths, weaknesses, opportunity, and threats. This was our chance to say, 'We are resetting.'*

*We've learned that there's the ability for some to work from home and more productively and to get a better work product. I think that we've also learned that there are others who can't work from home. I think that there were certain areas where maybe we were overstaffed. Maybe the way we've been working hasn't been the most efficient.*

*In the midst of all of this, we literally changed the brain of U.S. Stove, integrating a new ERP system. It's not that we needed any more challenges, but we were able to look at that and ask, 'What is it doing for us? Are we utilizing it? Did we buy a Ferrari, and we're only in second gear?'*

*That was actually my takeaway—we were only in second gear. I'm not saying we have to shift into sixth, but let's see what third and fourth feel like. And so we started working more effectively and more efficiently as a company.*

*The byproduct of that is that is to say, it's not throwing people a problem. It's throwing in good thought processes. It's improving efficiency. You could get the job done with the same amount of people, and then it's more profitable. I looked at it as a tremendous opportunity. I fully understand that the pandemic has been devastating to many families and businesses. I also see that for this company, it has been great.*

*As the year progressed, August saw the risks and bets that he took early in 2020 paid off in ways greater than even he could have imagined.*

*It became like a perfect storm. We had the latitude of our supply chain layered with the ability to take advantage of what we had seen other industries experiencing.*

*By the summer months, the supply chain from China had leveled out.*

*By fall, buyers started shifting their focus to our products. I pretty quickly started realizing that we actually hadn't ordered enough. Our demand was going to hugely outpace our ability to fulfill those orders. But just as quickly I was able to see because of the choices and moves we've made our company had been handed a loaded deck of cards where we were holding all the aces.*

*As our orders continued to soar, I called our key vendors and said, 'I want to convince you to send me millions of dollars of products. Here's the thing—I'm not going to pay you in advance. I'm basically buying your product on consignment.*

*I want you to front all of this. When we've produced and been paid for our products, I will pay you. And by the way, heads up, I'm going to come back and buy from you again.'*

*I've done that four times in three months, and our demand still exceeds our ability to supply. Just when you think it can't get crazier, we'll receive an order for $1 million from Amazon, and that's just a single day.*

*Our orders in the last quarter of 2020 have been up 400%.*

*Maybe some will make comparisons to other historic events that spiked our company's sales, like the Arab Oil Embargo in 1973. There were choices made during that time to expand. Many of those choices left U.S. Stove in a terrible over-extended position once the crisis passed.*

*I don't think we run the same risk today. We're simply living in a different technological era where data drives our decisions. It's real-time data vs. the kind of batch ordering my grandfather would have had to do. This is nothing like sticking a finger in the air and trying to guess which way the business winds are going to blow.*

*Our soaring demand at the end of 2020 is across the board, both brick and mortar and ecommerce customers.*

*The booming online business has created a whole new dynamic in interacting with the customer who is buying a product from U.S. Stove."*

# E-Commerce

Brandon:

*"In the past, people were traditionally going into a store, whether it's Lowe's, Home Depot, or Tractor Supply to buy a heater; now, they're going online. They're looking at reviews, which is challenging, because we try to make some of the more cost-effective products in the marketplace. And some people might have good reviews, and some people might have bad reviews. And that really plays a part in how we design our products for the future. We don't run from that, we seek it out, reaching out directly to the customer asking, 'Hey, I shipped you a product today. Can you tell me your direct feedback online through the retailer who sold it? Amazon.com, Homedepot.com, Wayfair, anybody like that? Please give me immediate feedback.' And we've never had that up until now, really.*

*Our industry is one of the last ones to jump into the online world, because it's a wood stove. You think a customer wants to look at it in person before they put it in their house. It's a piece of furniture. It's like walking into a furniture store, really, when it comes down to it. You don't buy much furniture online without seeing it. We're talking about something that's going to sit in the middle of your living space for the next 30 years. But people are getting more accustomed to that. It's an interesting shift.*

*There's this balancing act. We're going to have to be more reactive to direct customer feedback. Yet it's really hard to change ideas once they are established. These are certified products. If we change most any aspect of them, then we have to go back through recertification. So, it's a challenge. And I think that's going to be our hardest thing to fight in the future, is just that immediate feedback from the customer."*

August:
*"I think that the biggest challenges perpetuating the evolution of our business when it comes to transitioning from that brick-and-mortar into the e-commerce space is making sure we manage those e-tailers. We need to know our product placement. That innovation is going to continue and always has been a challenge for us, but it's one that we welcome, and that we now have the resources in place to support. We are focused on staying ahead of the curve and understanding the competitive landscape. It's one thing to know what you're doing. You obviously want to know what everybody else is doing, too.*

*Right now, our biggest challenge is literally managing this transition and business model. For years and years and years, we've been selling to the brick-and-mortar guys. All of a sudden, e-commerce became our biggest customer. I'm now selling to the consumer, not just to a corporate buyer.*

*We had one person buying for a lot of people. Now, we have a lot of people buying from one person, which is us. It's a complete 180.*

*Brandon also believes there will be an ongoing challenge of keeping folks interested in wood-burning heat."*

Brandon:

*"At the end of the day, wood heating requires work. You got to carry in the wood; if you're buying the firewood, you got to get it delivered to your house, or you deliver it to your house. You've got to stack it, you've got to season it. You've got to carry it in your house. You have to put it in your wood stove, you've got to clean your wood stove, there's ashes everywhere. So, it's not the cleanest process, and it requires a lot of work. While it's cheaper than a lot of other heating methods, it's work.*

*So, our challenge is that a lot of people are getting more used to just walking in and turning up a thermostat and less used to feeding a wood stove.*

*I think the challenge for our industry is the fact that we've got to make customers remember the nostalgia in wood heating, because wood heat has a comfort to it. If you ever sit in front of a wood stove, you know that it's a different type of heat than what's coming out of the register. You can feel that radiant heat off the glass. And so, there's the challenge of making people want wood heat for the experience and not just for heat."*

August:
*"We are embracing all these challenges. We have a great team. Our sales team, our engineering team, our operations, our supply chain, everybody literally from top to bottom. We have a great team in place that's willing to support all these transitions."*

## Updating the Brand

*Old U.S. Stove Company logo from early 1970's.*

August:
*"It's great that U.S. Stove is 150 years old. Old is good. Old is not good for a logo and company image. Our old image looked like the Ford emblem. In fact, I think that's pretty much where it's copied from. But as we approached the 150 years, I started to ask people in the company, myself included, Richard, 'What defines us? We're going to be 150 years old. What is our brand equity? What does it bring to the table?*

*Who knows us? Who doesn't know us?'*

*It turned out it was more a case of who doesn't know us. I took that as an opportunity to say, 'Let's reinvent the logo. Let's reinvent us as a company. Let's start following some of the same trajectory, the same path that other companies are on utilizing social media, getting brand exposure, brand awareness.' I was looking at the sales and marketing aspect of it.*

*One of the things that I learned is U.S. Stove is selling under all these different brands. Nobody knows who U.S. Stove is. I started asking people that had fireplaces, 'I know you know brands like Napoleon or Hearth and Home, but have you ever heard of U.S. Stove?' The reply was invariably, 'Never heard of them.' We've been around for 150 years, why shouldn't you know who we are?*

*And so, there was a lot of that, and I probably got a little more aggressive about it because of the simple fact that people hadn't heard of us. I'm extremely proud of the company for a lot of reasons. I want consumers to understand what we do. I want them to think of U.S. Stove when they need a new appliance or one of the many other products that we make.*

*We chose to engage some third-party marketing and PR firms. We reinvented the company as far as the logo and how we would go to market. We changed the website. We launched a new sub company, USSC Grills.*

*We also streamlined. At one time, I think we had as many as 45 brands out there. That's 45 different names, logos, and images. We consolidated all that down. Right now, we have United States Stove Company, which is going on everything. If ten years from now, you've purchased a pellet heater or wood stove, you want to be able to look on the back and be able to see that it's from U.S. Stove. It's not just an Ashley Brand, it's Ashley, but it's above all made by U.S. Stove Company.*

*Now we have the U.S. Stove brand, we have Ashley, which Richard acquired back in 1999. We have Vogelzang, an acquisition I was part of a few years back, USSC grills and Ranger, our forced air heater business. We've really streamlined and trimmed it down from the out-of-control list of 45 brands we started with."*

# 9

# FAMILY IS MORE THAN BLOOD

U.S. Stove is a family business, well beyond the generations of the Rogers family that have worked there. Many other families have brought in future generations, as well.

Richard Rogers says, "I think that originates back to my grandfather more than 80 years ago. He was a very family-oriented man. I would like to think this is a case of parents having a good experience and the next generation wanting to be involved with the company.

I believe in a lot of cases it goes back to a whole lot of pride, passion, the family thing. And it's not all about money of course. I mean we got to buy groceries and food, clothing and shelter, but I think there's a lot of it, a lot of that passion involved in our company. It is truly about loving your job."

The Cagle family agrees with that premise. James was the maintenance supervisor at U.S. Stove for 24 years. His son, Aaron, took over for him in 2014. Aaron explains the job, "We take care of all the building maintenance, all the machine maintenance, forklift maintenance, truck maintenance. Anything pretty much that goes wrong within the company, we do about 98% of it in house."

The Cagle family story actually goes back another generation. James' father worked at the company in the 1920s. Aaron says his grandfather worked in the U.S. Stove foundry. "They poured the iron and everything back when my grandfather worked here. They actually would pour and form and mold their own cast iron and things back in the day when my grandfather worked here."

*US Stove Company Employees (James' father, Ernest Cagle, is in the middle of the bottom row)*

Aaron worked as a contractor for many years, including some at U.S. Stove. The chance to work alongside his father, learn from him, and take over his position was one he just could not pass up. "I came to work for about six months with my dad. He trained me in the aspects of what he does, showing me all the ropes. Of course, I've worked with my dad my whole life, so it was neat to get to work with him at U.S. Stove, as well."

Both James and Aaron said the family leadership has made employees feel like family, as well. Aaron said, "I've worked for larger companies where you're basically just a number. Here, Richard knows my name. He knows where I live you know, and he's more like a family member, and, you know, a friend. In some of these big corporations, if you see the main guy out in town, he's not going to know who you are. But Richard knows most of those guys, and August, as well, on a first name basis probably nearly every guy that works in that plant."

Aaron talks about the value of family passing jobs onto the next generation. "I think a lot of people think that August got his job just because of who his family is. He's had to work to get there, and got the education to get there. I have faced the same thing. I've even had people make comments that I got my job because of my dad, who he was. Well, I mean that's probably right. I was qualified to get this job, because my dad trained me to know what I knew. This is what family business is about. I give U.S. Stove credit for hiring us as next-generation. A lot of places wouldn't even hire people that are in the same family."

Both father and son support the move to remove the union from U.S. Stove. James feels all the union business got in the way of running an efficient shop. Aaron says, "As a previous business owner myself, I wouldn't like the idea of somebody else telling me how to run my business and what I had to pay my employees and that sort of thing."

Longtime plant manager John Hargis was in charge when Aaron did contracting work for U.S. Stove. The Hargis family also has a multi-generational story with the company. John's brother, father, and uncle worked at the company, and when he turned eighteen, he decided to work there, as well.

His first job was loading trucks. He figures he had twenty or more jobs at the company since that time. In other words, he has done just about every job in the place except become president, though he certainly had a key role in shaping the current president, August Jones.

He likes to boast about August, "I once worked for his great grandfather. I worked for his grandfather. I worked for his uncles, Steve and Richard, and then, I babysat him."

August will be the first one to offer how much he has learned from John Hargis, including how to keep his cool during tense negotiations.

August:
*"You find yourself starting to overreact or get upset, before you say anything, walk back to the office calmly, breathe, decompress, and think about it, because the minute that you overreact, first of all, the people on the floor know that they've got you. And that they're in control, and you're likely going to say something that you can't take back, and then it exacerbates*

*the situation. He taught me a lot about that. There's a lot of the personnel stuff.*

*And then there's also a lot about learning our ERP system, financials as far as costed bills of materials. He essentially showed me how to cut my teeth on all that. He always managed to translate it into my next progression through the company, giving me the ability to see how all of the moving pieces from the very bottom go together.*

*John wasn't ever on the board of directors, so it would appear he had limited access to all the financial information, but I'm pretty sure he knew for the most part what those consisted of. And so, he kind of taught me the backend ropes on it."*

*John Hargis is clear that he made August earn his stripes. "And I gave him some rough jobs to start with. He didn't just come in and work in the office. He worked out in the plant. He's done everything out in the plant including all the dirty jobs. And then he knew what it took to run that plant. He knew who the people were, what they were going through in putting stuff together. He was always compliant doing the job I asked him to do for however long I asked him to do it."*

August says there were definite lows in his journey. "The worst was when I got stuck in the paint shop, because we had a supervisor there who couldn't do his job. I was soon doing the job better than that guy."

Hargis took some opportune times to give August his

promotions. There's the now famous story of how he instantly promoted August to Personnel Manager in the middle of overheated negotiations with union representatives.

That seemed to set the tone and style for bumping August up to the next level.

August:
*"We were looking at buying some straight side presses over near Lawrenceburg. The guy we were dealing with asked us for our business cards. This guy, of course, he's VP of manufacturing. I handed him my business card, and he did a double take. He's this old guy wearing overalls, a very country guy. He just asks, 'What is a personnel manager doing here looking at machinery?'*

*John looked at me and said, 'We need to get you another title.'*

*I said, 'What title should I get?' I didn't have any idea.*

*That was the moment I became Director of Manufacturing Operations.*

*All of my titles worked like that, I mean with the exception of president. They were all impromptu leading up to that just kind of off the cuff."*

Hargis agrees, "I knew Richard would be OK with it, because giving a promotion doesn't cost any money. I didn't promise him a raise, just a bigger title."

When it was time to talk money, Hargis doesn't admit

this, but August says he was in there going to bat for him. "He was more than fair and generous when it came to going to bat for me from a standpoint of compensation, because he would have meetings with Richard. And Richard really leaned on him a lot as far as what I should or shouldn't get. John always got me more than I thought I would have ever gotten every step of the way, every progression, and conversation along the way."

The one catch? August has long been expected to buy his own lunch.

As it became clear that August was getting ready to step into the president's chair, John Hargis took it as the cue that his work at U.S. Stove was pretty much done. He could finally retire.

August knew exactly who he wanted to fill the role, a man he didn't know well, but John Hargis sure did.

Gerald Hargis remembers getting the phone call. "I had never talked to August before. I knew August through Dad and back and forth. But as far as talking, we had never spoken. Dad never said anything about it. August called me on the phone and started asking me if I was interested in maybe coming to U.S. Stove. He asked me if I'd come down and talk to him. And I came down, brought a resume down to him, and we talked. Everything kind of just clicked."

August jumps in to share his take on this part of the story.

August:

*"There's a back story to this. Around this time with the progression of the company, there were some changes in our overall upper management.*

*Richard and I had started having more discussions about my future and where I was going. Everybody understood that I was on this trajectory to eventually step into the role that I'm in today.*

*It had started moving more rapidly, and I started going up to the corporate office spending more time up there. As Richard started calling me up, I became privy to the financials. He explained to the CFO at that time that he wanted me to be aware of everything. He said, 'I want August to be aware of everything. There is nothing I want you to hide.'*

*I could see every salary in the company, from those who made more than me to those who made less.*

*Of course, John never missed a beat. He realized what was going on. I'll never forget I came back to the office he and I had been sharing. John had built this office himself. There was my space, which was like an 8x5 shoebox with a desk and room for not much else. There was a door between our spaces. Of course, his space was much bigger than mine.*

*As I walked in our office that day, he looked at me and said, 'Listen, Big Boy, if you're moving up, I'm moving out.'*

*One of the agreements that I had with him, whether spoken or unspoken, was when I was coming in to take his shoes, fill his role; he could retire, and then from there, I would move up.*

*Everything kind of started happening more quickly. We all knew I wasn't going to stay in the role of vice president of manufacturing for long. One morning, I was in Chattanooga, and I was taking a shower, and this light bulb just goes off. And none of the candidates that I talked to had seemed to fit.*

*All of the sudden, I thought about Gerald. He was in manufacturing. He'd been with Komatsu for 25 years. He knew welding and sheet metal. He had a legacy to the company.*

*He came down. I sat in John's chair. Gerald was probably sitting in the same chair I sat in when I interviewed.*

*He handed me his resume, and I took it and tossed it in the trash can. I said, 'I don't need a piece of paper that tells me anything about you.' I already know everything I need to know about you. All I need to know now is would you be willing to sit in this chair? This is your dad's chair.'*

*And he said, 'Yes I'd love the opportunity.'"*

*Richard Rogers, John Hargis, August Jones, and Gerald Hargis. 2021. Credit: Jessica Pope.*

John Hargis:
*"It really was when I could see August and Gerald, both were going to be all set in their new roles that I felt I could leave. I spent a lot of years taking care of this company, worrying about this company. When August took over and then Gerald came in, I figured I had nothing more to worry about. I could go. I could retire."*

*The full story is that word around U.S. Stove is John Hargis has never really completely left. His official title is now, "Consultant." August says it's the latest round of the ongoing games with titles. "We just changed his title and reduced his pay. He's still around though. And probably will be forever."*

# 10

# THE WOMEN

It would be a mistake to assume the success of U.S. Stove is all due to the men of the family. There are key women in this story who made the success possible.

There was Mary Francis Raulston Rogers, who kicked her young son out of their home separating him from his abusive father, and by her own account, saving the lives of her son and husband.

S.L. Rogers's first wife, Amanda Raulston, made up for his limited education, teaching him to read and write, giving him the manners and ability to impress society.

*Ruth Parham Rogers; aka "Mama"*

Ruth Parham Rogers, despite her challenges with her mental health, gave S.L. Rogers, Sr. the family he'd always wanted. The four children she birthed and raised went on to create the generations of family who have brought the U.S. Stove Company successfully into the 21st century.

Had this story unfolded decades later, perhaps instead of her son, it would have been her oldest daughter, Emmy, taking over the business. She was ahead of her time as a woman who enjoyed working and business.

> Reece:
> *"My mother always worked. She ran Marion Lumber Company and Marion Finance Company. She'd go to work at nine o'clock. My father would pick her up at noon every day. They'd come home to eat lunch. Then, he'd drop her off at the Lumber Company again, and he'd probably go play golf."*

Perhaps, had this been a time when it wasn't automatically assumed a son should take over the father's business, Leonard would've been free to pursue his true passions and callings, and his sister, Emmy, would have thrived as a business leader.

## Ruth Rogers Wainwright

*"Little" Ruth Parham Rogers.*

As the last surviving child of SL Rogers, Sr. Ruth Rogers Wainwright has become the matriarch of the family. The respect she garners from the family is about more than simply living into her 80s. It's about what she's done with her life. She became a wife, mother, and grandmother. She became an ordained minister.

*Ruth Rogers Wainwright and her husband, Tom Wainwright. 2021. Credit: Jessica Pope.*

Perhaps, most importantly, she became the family leader and example in talking about mental illness. She says, "Just like my mother, I am bipolar."

Ruth has dedicated much of her life to talking about mental illness and the power of medication. She has spoken openly and honestly with various family members—encouraging them to seek help, like she has.

Her counsel comes from a place of love and of knowing the possibility of making things better. "Bipolar is in our genes. Actually, some of the smartest people in history were bipolar. High intelligence seems to go with it. If it's watched for early and treated early, we can have a good, productive life. I mean, I'm evidence of that. But if it goes untreated, it can ultimately lead to schizophrenia and suicide. We don't want that to happen anymore."

## Anne White Forrester Rogers

*Anne Forrester Rogers*

There's a little-known heroine of the story when it comes to the chapter of Richard and Steve fighting to save the U.S. Stove Company. First, they had to get control of the company. Their own mother, Anne White Forrester Rogers, played a key role, even though she and Leonard Rogers were divorced at the time of his death.

Steve:
*"We wouldn't have had ownership in the company without our mother's help. She had ended up with what was worthless stock in the company as part of the divorce settlement.*

*My dad's second wife had visions of taking over the company. She had two children, and she wanted them to run the company.*

*All the stock was in my dad's estate, and I was the trustee of the estate. Richard and I were co-executors. In order to get the stock out of the estate where she couldn't get her hands on it, I went to my mother and said that I need $100,000 dollars to put into the estate.*

*We are going to take the stock out. Richard and I are going to own the stock. She didn't have a whole lot of money, but after she thought about it for a period of time, she talked to John Stoffel, her attorney. I don't know if he advised her against it or for it. You couldn't blame him if he did advise against it. A 30-and 25-year old kid coming and wanting $100,000 when all you have left is $250,000 at 75 years old is not the best move. I mean who* *will do that if not your sons? And she did it.*

*We put the money into the estate and got stock out. Betty couldn't get her hands on it. Before that transaction was approved, we had an attorney.*

*We had to go to court. Betty's attorney put me up on the stand. I had letters from all the vendors we owed a bunch of money and the banks and all this stuff to prove that this stock was worthless, which it was. We were able to establish that $100,000 was a reasonable amount to give in exchange for the stock. It worked, and Richard and I got control of the company. Without our mother's help, that would've never happened, and this would've been a very different story."*

## The Earrings

Ruth shares a beautiful story that links the Rogers women through five generations and beyond.

Ruth:
*"My father's first wife, Amanda, had a pair of earrings. They were small earrings made of onyx featuring a small diamond in the middle of each one. When my two older sisters were teenagers, my parents had those earrings made into rings.*

*Since Emmy went on to have three sons and no daughters, when I was in my teens, she gave me her ring. When my oldest granddaughter, Stephanie, turned sixteen, I passed on the ring to her."*

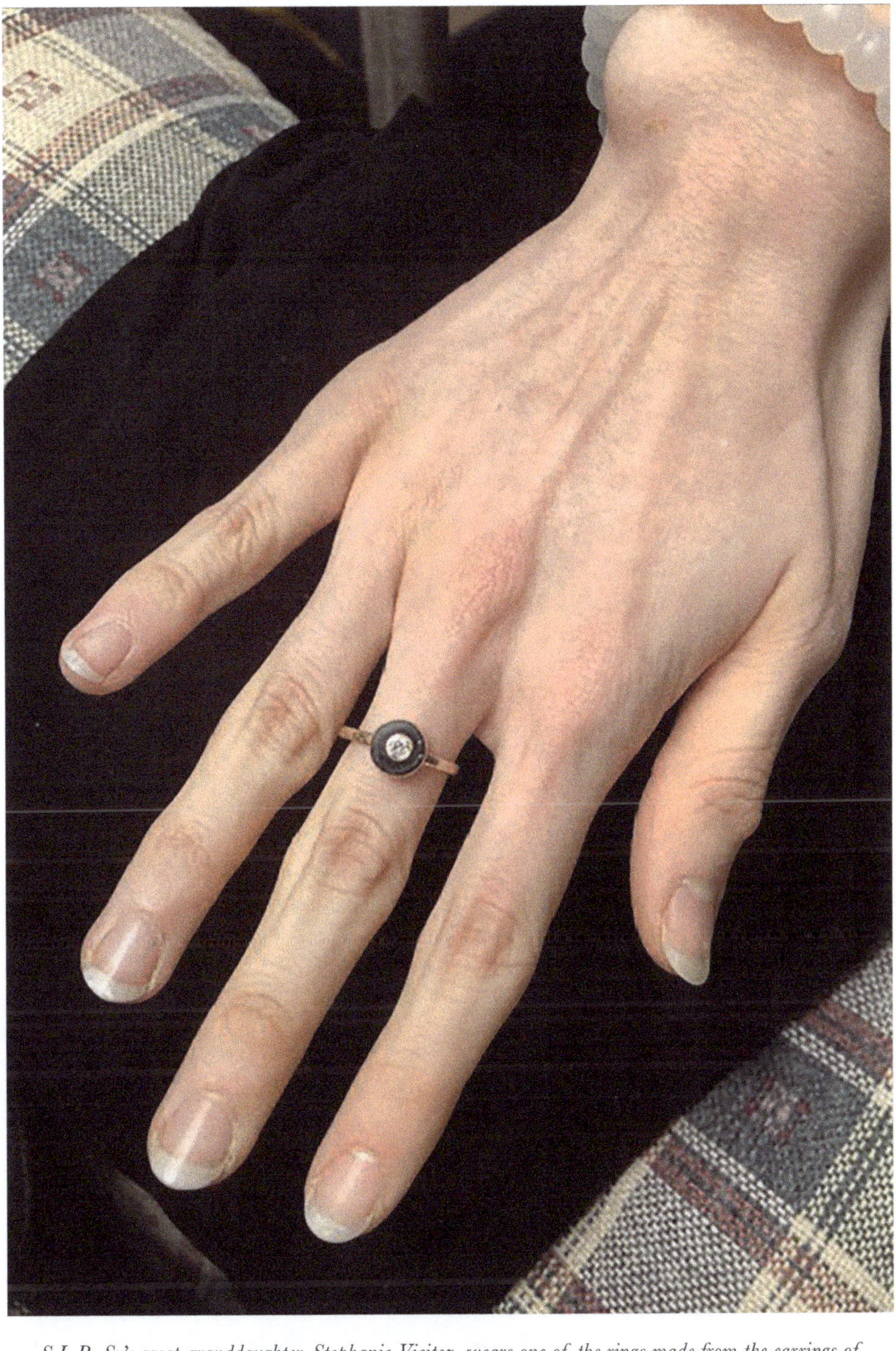

*S.L.R, Sr's great-granddaughter, Stephanie Vieitez, wears one of the rings made from the earrings of Amanda Rogers.*

These two wives, Amanda and Ruth, never knew each other. Yet, my mother felt it important to always honor Amanda, their connection, and her part in this family. That honor will keep reaching through the generations tying their descendants back to two remarkable women.

# 11

# THE FUTURE

*Descendants of S.L. Rogers, Sr. and Ruth Parham Rogers gather in South Pittsburg, TN. 2016.*

U.S. Stove is an ever-changing company and story. Attorney and longtime Rogers family friend, Harvey Cameron, says this is a story of survival. "It goes back to S.L. Rogers, Sr.; Lenny also did a lot to make the company survive. It has been a company that has evolved by changing their types of stoves and how they do business."

Despite the incredible story of four generations of the same family running the company, there has never been any guarantee that U.S. Stove would remain family-run and owned.

Just like his father before him, Richard once seriously considered selling the company. He says, "I got to the point that I understood how my father had felt trapped. I didn't appear to have anybody in the family that had the expertise or interest to take it over. In 2006, a company came in and made me a hell of an offer. It was going to be all cash at closing. Anybody with half a brain would have said, 'Yes.'"

August was already working at the company and took the attempted buyout as a real wake-up call. He says, "I remember walking the top executives from this potential buyer through our manufacturing facility. There was this one guy who was especially arrogant who I had to walk around. I knew the moment these people would take over my job at U.S. Stove would be over."

A couple factors eventually helped to kill the deal. Richard says the interested buyers started changing the terms of the offer. "It went from all cash to an earn-out situation where I kept working several more years. I finally came to the conclusion, 'Why would I want to work for them to make money for them so that they could pay me?'"

They also started showing interest in a U.S. Stove competitor that found itself struggling. "Harman Stoves was choked up with too much inventory and not enough cash. The U.S. Stove buyer suddenly decided it was a better investment in Harman rather than U.S. Stove."

August gets emotional thinking back on when the deal fell through. "I had always worked hard, but seeing this opportunity almost disappear, it made me work even harder. And yet, even today, I still remember that this could all be taken away."

There was some sweet payback a couple years later. August and Richard got wind that the same company that had played with buying U.S. Stove was making a move to buy another company. The acquiring company had done all the due diligence and all the work to close the deal.

Richard remembers how he called up the guy from the private equity group who was handling the deal. "I asked, 'What do we got to do to just buy this damn thing?' He told me a number, and I said, 'Well, let's just do it.'

We snuck in like thieves in the night.

Six days. The law firm gave us a "Quickest Closing Award."

August remembers a moment of sweet revenge. "I ran into that same arrogant son of a bitch at the airport. After stealing it away from him like thieves in the night, I just looked at him knowing we had closed the deal after they had done all the work and said, 'It is really nice to see you again.'"

Ruth gets such joy from hearing these kinds of stories.

She makes sure to tell Richard and August, "Papa is so proud of you guys. These kinds of stories feel like hearing him talk about something he has done to close a deal or steal it out from somebody. You've definitely got the genes."

## Ownership

From the time Richard bought out his brother, Steve, he owned 100% of the U.S. Stove Company. As August rose through the ranks and eventually started running the company, both men understood there were some big conversations for them to have.

August:
*"There's the bigger picture, where I think we both recognize that U.S. Stove is something bigger than just him, it's bigger than just me, and it's something that is a phenomenal opportunity that just doesn't exist for many companies: 150 years, four generations and a fifth sitting there in cue.*

*The conversation was not really much of a conversation. It was more like, 'How do I start transitioning ownership to you?' Because I think that is his intention, to shift it to me, just at some point my intention is going to be to shift it to the fifth generation.*

*It's gradual. My ownership stake has grown to 10%, and it's likely to grow from there. None of this was ever a done deal simply because I'm Richard's nephew. There have been plenty of people who have tried to carve me out and block my path as I used hard work to progress my way through the company. My current position leading the company is a result of my hard work and Richard believing in me."*

August has long understood Richard's vision. "He wanted to be able to be sitting at the beach and call me up and ask me how the business is running and I'm running it. I remember the first time he called me from the beach, and I was actually sitting at his desk. I couldn't help thinking, 'Here we are.'

This year, 2020, that came true more than we ever expected, as Richard rode out much of the pandemic at his beach condo in Florida. Those phone calls weren't for a weekend. It was for the whole damn year."

"It was no longer a situation of my calling an employee. August is a co-owner."

As of late 2020, Richard shared the news that he has transferred 49% ownership of U.S. Stove to August. He holds the remaining 51%.

## The Fifth Generation

As for future leaders of the U.S. Stove Company, it appears lessons have been learned. Steve put a stop to one ongoing family tradition. There is no S.L. Rogers IV. Steve had all girls, but even if he had a son, he was resolute that he would not pass on the name of father and grandfather.

> Steve:
> *"No. That kind of name puts a child in a box. This is what you are supposed to do. It's a bigger world today."*

No descendant of S.L. Rogers, Sr. will be forced into the family business. That's not to say there are not budding businessmen and women growing up in the fifth generation.

Remember Richard's story of getting the cigar box and those first lessons about money from his grandfather, SLR, Sr.? Richard has made sure the tradition continues.

> Richard:
> *"This past Christmas, I gave that exact gift to several children. I went to the cigar place in Chattanooga on Cherry Street and got a bunch of empty cigar boxes. I think I paid $1 a piece for them, and gave them out for Christmas with a note, a handwritten note with it—with each one of them about the story of getting this kind of cigar box from my grandfather. And so, hopefully, possibly it will have the*

*same kind of influence on some of these other children that it made on me."*

*S.L.R, Sr.'s great-grandson, August Jones with his children, Ayden, Austen, and Autumn Jones. 2021. Credit: Jessica Pope*

As for August, who is he thinking of when he mentions the fifth generation?

August:
*"I don't want to pigeonhole it to just my children, because they are still young, and who knows what they will want to do?*

*Also, I know Richard has a grandson. I wouldn't want to limit the opportunity to just my three kids simply because I'm in leadership now. I want to make sure that the landscape is open, and it's not this nepotistic view that I have to bring in my oldest son.*

*I think even from the standpoint of my oldest son, I think he would love to do it, I think he would be proud to do it, he wants to make me proud, but at the same time, I want him to pursue whatever career he wants to.*

*I think that by not forcing it and allowing that landscape to kind of develop, I think the fifth generation is going to come on, whoever that's going to be, and do great.*

*It could even be my youngest, my daughter. I'd say with her sass and spunk and how she carries herself, she would be a definite possibility. But again, the most important thing with the fifth generation is not to force it."*

# The Conversation He'd Love to Have

It's the thing money can't buy. August would love to have a conversation with the man who started it all, his great-grandfather, S.L. Rogers, Sr.

August:

*"I'd love to share in his experience. From him running the coal mines in Jasper, Tennessee, to being the mayor of South Pittsburg, and of course, his days running U.S. Stove. I'd love to hear his story of 1937, feeling the pressure of stepping into the position of taking over this company that was the wheelhouse for a local economy coming to the rescue of this community.*

*I would ask him what it was like to take on this challenge of literally supporting an entire community. I would want to know how he managed grocery stores and all his other businesses. He seemed to be just kind of a jack of all trades and a master of all, too.*

*I would love to just be able to sit down and hear some of the specifics of his different business ventures and what he got involved in and what made him tick. What were the pros and cons, what were the upsides? Why did you like this particular business better than you like this one? What's the fun part of it? Because I always love to be profitable, I love to make money, but I'd love to love doing it, too. My understanding of him was that he loved to do it, too.*

*I just really wish I had gotten to know him."*

Though he knew his grandfather, Richard, too, would like one more conversation. He'd love to share all that has happened in the last 60 years. What would his grandfather think of the triumphs? Of the tragedies?

One thing Richard is certain of, S.L. Rogers, Sr. would be proud.

Richard:

*"I think he'd be very proud to know what we've done, how we've done. It started with him, with the biggest gift he gave all of us, the only thing any of us were ever promised. He gave us the opportunity.*

*In addition to opportunity, he gave us a great reputation. That's because he was a great man! I graciously salute my grandfather, S.L.R., Sr. and the wonderful heritage he passed to all of us!"*

*Stephen Leonard & Ruth Parham Rogers' Descendants with partners*

*David Dame Rogers (Father of Stephen L. Rogers, Sr.)*

*Stephen Leonard Rogers, Sr.*

*Ruth Parham Rogers*

*S.L.R., Sr. and Ruth Rogers in the side yard of the "Big House."*

*Ruth Parham Rogers & Stephen Leonard Rogers, Sr. with daughter, Ruth Parham Rogers.*

*Ruth Parham Rogers' playhouse. S.L.R., Sr. had it built for her on the family farm.*

*Stephen Leonard Rogers, Jr, Nancy Jane Rogers, Ruth Parham Rogers & Emma Lockert Rogers*

*First grandchild, Stephen L. Rogers III, Summer 1950.*

*S.L. Rogers, Sr. makes sure to capture a precious moment with oldest grandson, Steve (Stephen L. Rogers III).*

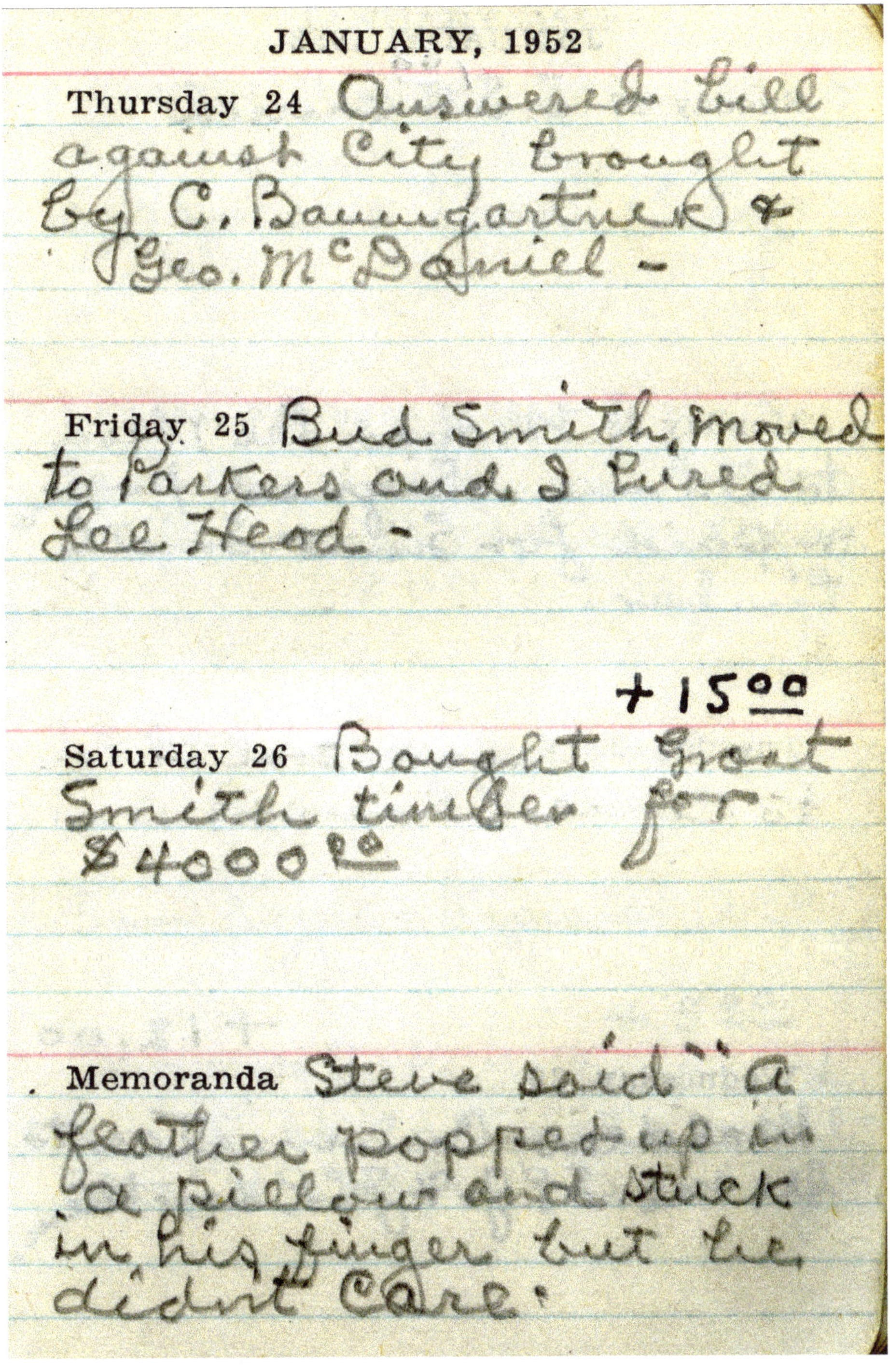

JANUARY, 1952

Thursday 24 Answered bill against City brought by C. Baumgartner & Geo. McDaniel -

Friday 25 Bud Smith moved to Parkers and I hired Lee Head -

+ 15.00

Saturday 26 Bought Grant Smith timber for $4000.00

Memoranda Steve said "a feather popped up in a pillow and stuck in his finger but he didnt care."

*Stephen Leonard Rogers, Sr. diary entry in 1952. about Stephen Leonard Rogers, III*

*Rogers siblings Steve, Richard, Julie, and Carolyn. 1955.*

*S.L.R. Rogers, Sr. holds grandson, Reece Thomas, as oldest grandson S.L.Rogers III, stands beside him.*

*SL Rogers, III, Betty Turner, Reece Thomas, SL Rogers, Sr., Julia W. Rogers & Carolyn Rogers*

*Father, Grandfather, Christian, Businessman, & Politician: Stephen Leonard Rogers, Sr.*

*Anne (White) Forrester Rogers*

*Anne White Forrester & Stephen Leonard Rogers, Jr.'s Wedding Day, December 27, 1947, in Union City, Tennessee.*

*Brothers Steve, Bill, and Richard Rogers. 1960.*

*Ruth Rogers, February 1964.*

*Leonard Rogers and his three sons, Steve, Richard, Bill. Easter 1967.*

*The five Rogers children: Richard, Steve, Carolyn, Julia, and Bill. 1962.*

*The Rogers Family: Julia, Richard, Carolyn, Steve, mother Anne, and Bill. South Pittsburg, TN. 1984.*

*Grandson Bill Rogers pursuing a favorite past time of drinking coffee. It often inspired him as he wrote poetry.*

*Steve Rogers and mother, Anne. Christmas, 1984.*

*Steve Rogers (SLR, III) finishing Battlefield Marathon, 1983*

*Steve, Bill and Richard, the three Rogers brothers clowning around, Christmas, 1988.*

*Richard Rogers and son, Stephen Richard "Rock" Rogers. 2021. Credit: Jessica Pope.*

*Great-great-grandson of S.L. Rogers, Sr., Sam Turner, Steve Rogers, and Sam's father, Richard Turner. 2021.*

*S.L. Rogers, Sr.'s granddaughter, Julia Rogers. 2021. Credit: Jessica Pope.*

*S.L. Rogers, Sr.'s grandson, Steve, and his daughter, Stephanie Rogers Esper. Stephanie is the family genealologist.*

*Siblings Richard Rogers, Julia Rogers, and Steve Rogers. 2021 Credit: Jessica Pope.*

*The five children of Nancy Rogers and Paul Turner: Amy, Richard, Nancy Ann, Paul, Jr., and Betty.*

*S.L. Rogers, Sr.'s great-granddaughter, Christie Jones and her mother, Julia Rogers. 2021. Credit: Jessica Pope.*

*Stephen Richard "Rock" Rogers, great grandson of S.L. Rogers, Sr. Son of Richard Rogers. 2020*

*Richard, his daughter Chanel and fiancée Kaye Stafford , 2019 in California.*

*Ruth Rogers Wainwright's family. L to R: Mary Lee Wainwright, Ruth, husband Tom, and Kelly Ruth Wainwright Vieitez.*

*Richard Rogers and fiancee, Kaye Stafford. 2021. Credit: Jessica Pope.*

*Great-great grandson of S.L.R. Sr., Barrett Bumgarner, with his mother, Stephanie Rogers Esper. 2009.*

*Jonas Connor, great-great grandson of S.L. Rogers, Sr. 2021. Credit: Jessica Pope.*

*Elena and Stephanie Vieitez, great granddaughters of S.L.R., Sr. Granddaughters of Ruth Rogers Wainwright.*

*Richard Rogers and grandson, River Rogers. 2021. Credit: Jessica Pope.*

# ACKNOWLEDGMENTS

This book does not have a single author. It is a compilation of memories, thoughts, and opinions from family members, employees, and historians.

Special thanks to all the descendants of S.L. Rogers, Sr., employees of U.S. Stove Company, and friends of the family who so generously shared their time, memories, and insights in the summer and fall months of 2020.

Special thanks to Richard Rogers, who financed and instigated the project; Stephanie Rogers Esper, who, long before this book began, started her extensive research that built the family tree as seen on page 274.

Rodger Castleberry, who pushed through physical illness and pain to share stories and perspectives only he knows.

David Head, Marion County Hustler for his historical articles.

Carolyn Millhiser at the South Pittsburg Historical Society for her invaluable research assistance.

And all the future descendants of S.L. Rogers, Sr. and U.S. Stove employees who care about this family, this company, and our story as it continues to unfold for generations to come.

Amanda L Rogers (1876-1922)

Stephen L Rogers Sr. (1882-1965)

Ruth Parham Rogers (1898-1980)

Emma L Rogers (1927-1989)

Nancy Jane Rogers (1930-2005)

Ruth Rogers Wainwright (1939-Living)

Stephen Rogers III (1949-Living)

Julia White Rogers (1950-Living)

Carolyn Rogers (1951-2009)

Anne Forrester Rogers (1924-2016)

Stephen L Rogers Jr. (1925-1979)

Betty W Rogers (1925-2019)

Richard B Rogers (1954-Living)

William F Rogers (1955-2012)

A

Emma L
Rogers
(1927-1989)

Robert Reece
Thomas Sr.
(1923-2019)

William R
Thomas
(1950-1950)

Robert R
Thomas
(1952-Living)

David L
Thomas
(1953-Living)

Frank Rogers
Thomas
(1956-2015)

B

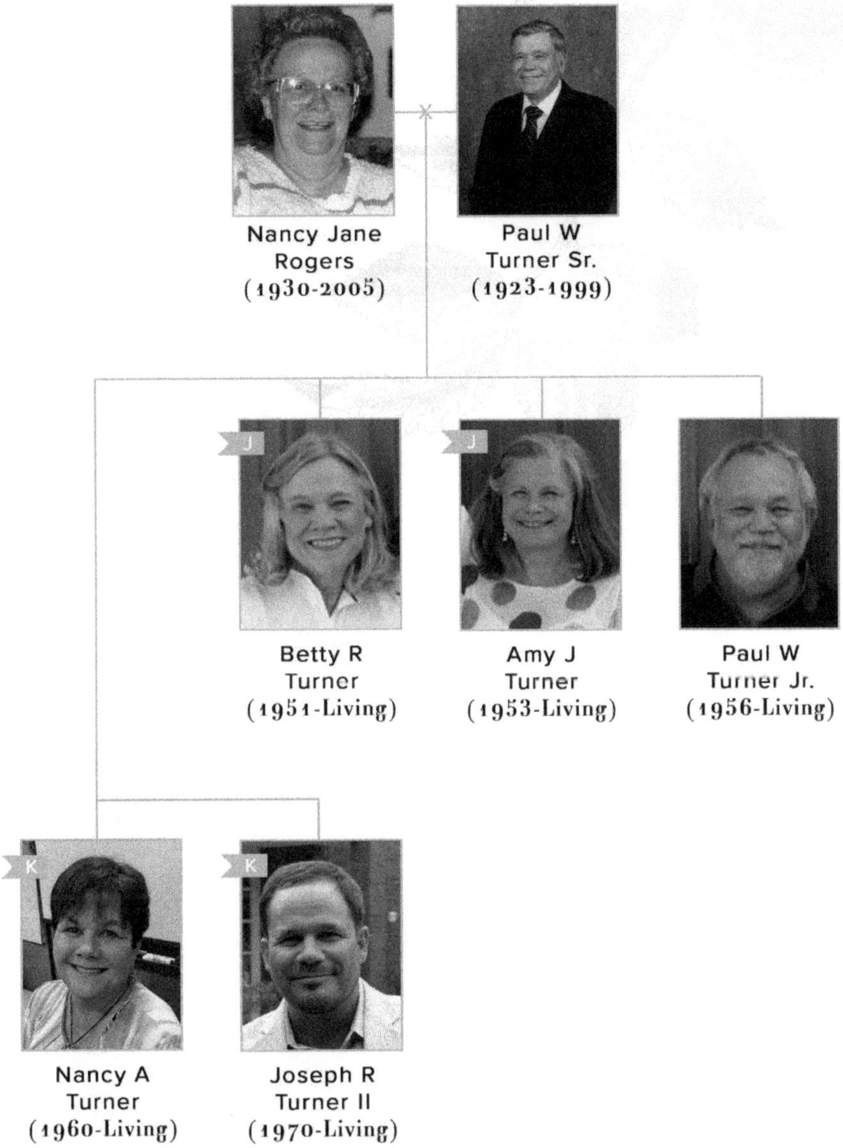
Nancy Jane
Rogers
(1930-2005)
Paul W
Turner Sr.
(1923-1999)
J
Betty R
Turner
(1951-Living)
J
Amy J
Turner
(1953-Living)
Paul W
Turner Jr.
(1956-Living)
K
Nancy A
Turner
(1960-Living)
K
Joseph R
Turner II
(1970-Living)

C

Catherine C Griffin (Living)

Stephen L Rogers III (1949-Living)

Christine H Rogers (1950-Living)

Casey B Bumgarner (1973-Living)

Stephanie R Rogers Esper (1973-Living)

Matthew P Esper (1969-Living)

William Barrett Bumgarner (2004-Living)

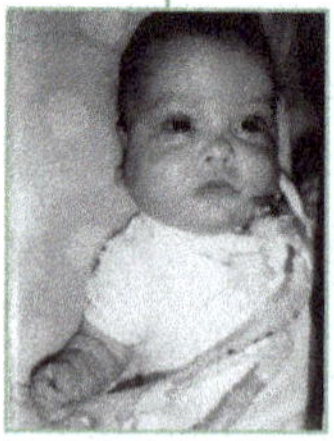

Stephen Brock Bumgarner (2006-2006)

Michael J Cox (1976-Living)
Stacey M Rogers Cox (1975-Living)
Kristina M Kulesz (1979-Living)
Amanda R Rogers (1977-Living)
Christian P Cox (2004-Living)
Lauren M Cox (2007-Living)
Jacob B Kulesz (2009-Living)

D

Ruth Rogers
Wainwright
(1939-Living)

Tom A
Wainwright
(1938-Living)

Constantino
Vieitez
(1959-Living)

Kelly Wainwright
Vieitez
(1966-Living)

Mary Lee
Wainwright
(1969-Living)

Stephanie
Vieitez
(2003-Living)

Elena
Vieitez
(2009-Living)

E

John Guider (Living)
Julia White Rogers (1950-Living)
Samuel R Jones Jr (1952-Living)
Christie E Jones (1977-Living)
Sam Paul Jones II (1982-Living)
Stephen L Jones (1984-Living)
August S L Jones (1979-Living)
Kayla Powers Jones (1984-Living)
Ayden S L Jones (2009-Living)
Austen R A Jones (2015-Living)
Autumn A Jones (2018-Living)

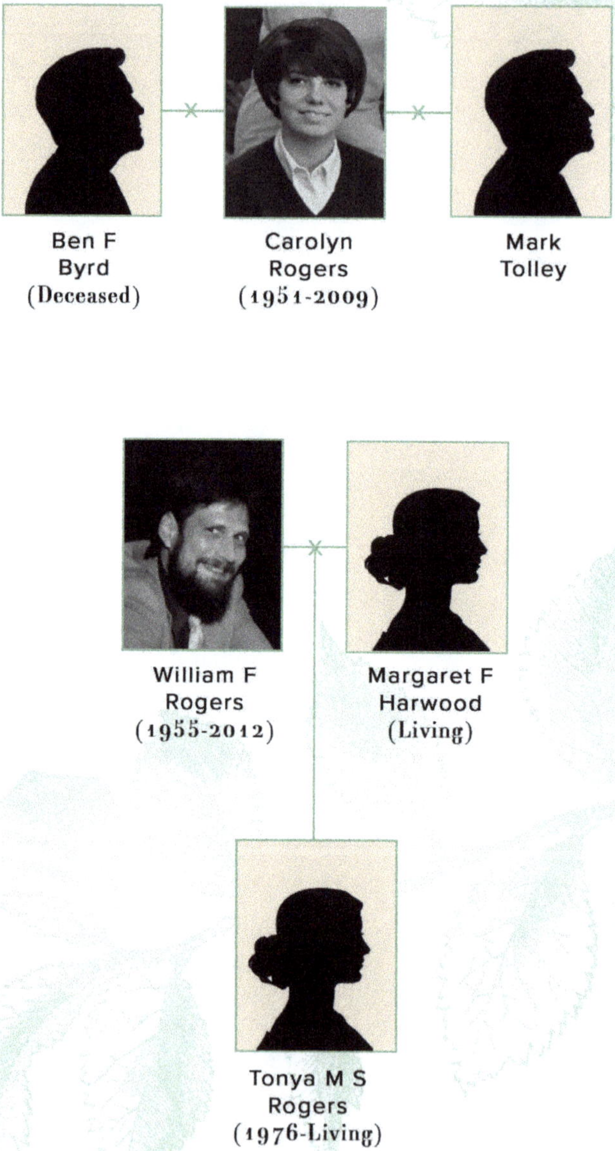
Ben F
Byrd
(Deceased)
Carolyn
Rogers
(1951-2009)
Mark
Tolley
William F
Rogers
(1955-2012)
Margaret F
Harwood
(Living)
Tonya M S
Rogers
(1976-Living)

G

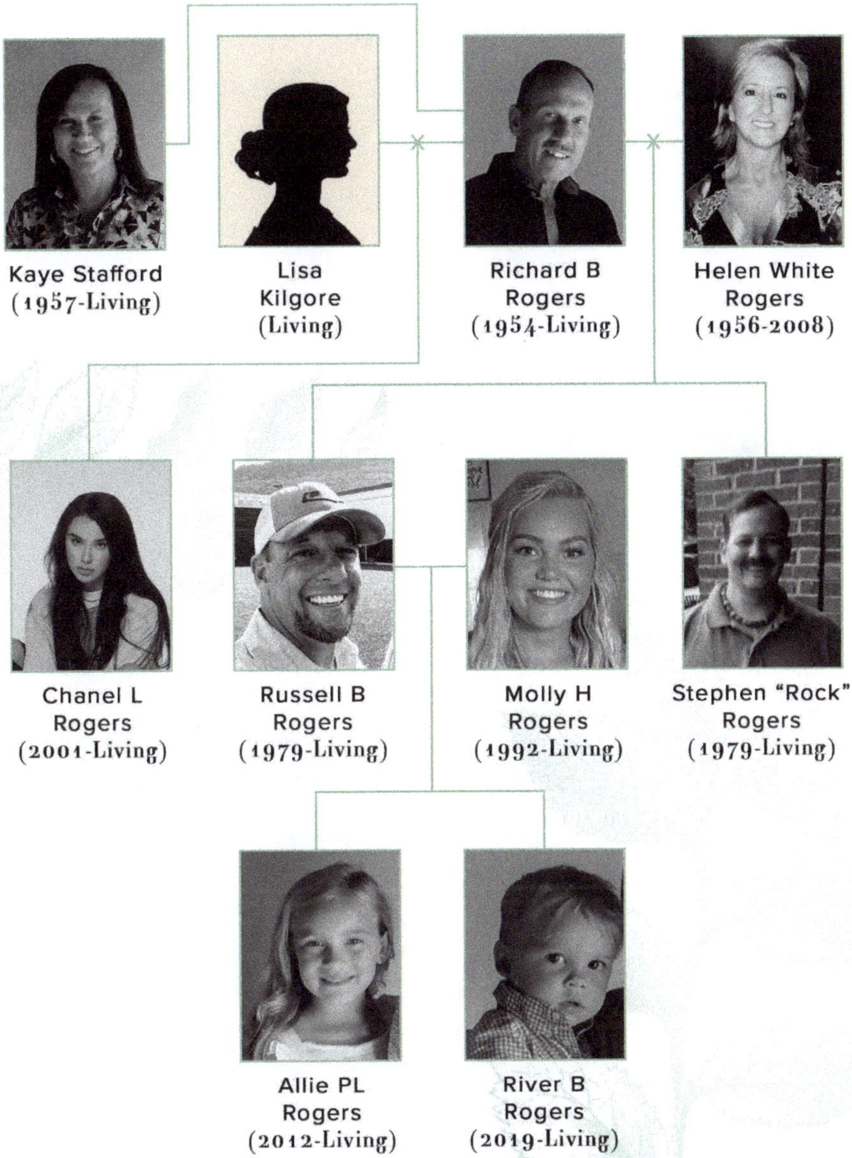
Kaye Stafford
(1957-Living)
Lisa
Kilgore
(Living)
Richard B
Rogers
(1954-Living)
Helen White
Rogers
(1956-2008)
Chanel L
Rogers
(2001-Living)
Russell B
Rogers
(1979-Living)
Molly H
Rogers
(1992-Living)
Stephen "Rock"
Rogers
(1979-Living)
Allie PL
Rogers
(2012-Living)
River B
Rogers
(2019-Living)

H

Jennifer L Simpson (1971-Living)
Robert R Thomas (1952-Living)
Sandra Y Giddens (1963-Living)
Zackrey R Woods (1987-Living)
Jennifer L T Woods (1987-Living)
Robert R Thomas III (1989-Living)
Carl R Thomas (1990-Living)
Elanor R Woods (2021-Living)
Thomas R Woods (2021-Living)
Ansleigh L Thomas (2013-Living)
Grayson B Thomas (2016-Living)
Blake Boyd Thomas (1983-2013)
Emma C Thomas (2001-Living)

Frank Rogers Thomas (1956-2015)
Robin Kay Rogers (1957-Living)
Stephen B Thomas (1981-Living)
Leona Marie Precilla (1985-Living)
Allen Stuart Thomas (1984-Living)
Monica L Thomas (1989-Living)
Shanna R Thomas (1986-2014)
Patton R Thomas (2020-Living)
Henry F Thomas (2019-Living)
Hudson R Thomas (2021-Living)

J

Bob
Burns

Amy J
Turner
(1953-Living)

James Aulton
Parker

Andrew
Bronneck
(1977-Living)

Margaret P
Bronneck
(1979-Living)

Andrew J
Bronneck
(2015-Living)

Emma L
Bronneck
(2018-Living)

Betty R
Turner
(1951-Living)

Gary Paul
Kane
(1943-Living)

Sophia P T
Kane
(1994-Living)

Katherine R
Kane
(1996-Living)

K

Nancy A Turner (1960-Living)
Clifton C Hookey Sr (1960-Living)
Joseph R Turner II (1970-Living)
Mary Ann Sanders Turner (1970-Living)
Nancy K H Conner (1983-Living)
Clifton Hookey Jr (1986-2021)
Joseph T Hookey (1992-Living)
Samuel P R Turner (2000-Living)
Abbey Kate Conner (2007-Living)
Jonas Gray Conner (2009-Living)
Olivia Rose Hookey (2013-Living)

Although the content of this book may seem pretty simple and straightforward, let it be known that there were many, many hours by many, many caring individual family and friend members to make this truly the result of a labor of love.

It is my hope and dream that this edition will inspire future generations to value our heritage as much as those involved in this printed edition.

It is the future generations that are writing the next edition and I have great hopes and expectations that they will glean some good lessons from our family history that would otherwise be unknown if not for this humble undertaking.

I certanly value my heritage and the blessings that have been bestowed on my family and each and all of the descendants of SLR, Sr.

Sincerely and with the Upmost Humility,

Richard Rogers
Proud descendant of SLR, Sr.

StoryTerrace

CPSIA information can be obtained
at www.ICGtesting.com
Printed in the USA
LVHW072159060822
724765LV00001B/1

9 798986 221519